MANAGING URBAN GOVERNMENT SERVICES

James L. Mercer
Susan W. Woolston
William V. Donaldson

In the 1980s local government administrators will be forced to operate under conditions radically different from those that prevailed in the last two decades. The 60s were the decade of federal largesse, with expanding revenues, responsibilities, and opportunities for local government. Now it appears that the 70s were a transitional period when reality, primarily in the form of inflation, declining revenues, high energy costs, and citizen cynicism, began to curtail local government initiatives. Expectations about what government might accomplish not only stopped growing, but, to some extent, even reversed themselves. Citizens began to view government negatively—as part of the problem, offering no solutions.

The current cost/revenue squeeze will probably continue and may even worsen in the years ahead, and local government will be forced to manage with reduced resources and revenue—a formidable task for any organization. This book is designed to help managers in local government cope with the challenges they face. The coverage is broad and touches on virtually every service area that a local government manager has within purview. Reflecting the realities of the political environment, the discussion is pragmatic and ranges from suggestions on how to organize local government operations for greater efficiency to actual case examples that demonstrate the application of cost-saving systems and technology by local government units.

MANAGING
URBAN GOVERNMENT
SERVICES

MANAGING
URBAN GOVERNMENT
SERVICES

STRATEGIES, TOOLS, AND TECHNIQUES
FOR THE EIGHTIES

JAMES L. MERCER
SUSAN W. WOOLSTON
WILLIAM V. DONALDSON

A DIVISION OF AMERICAN MANAGEMENT ASSOCIATIONS

Library of Congress Cataloging in Publication Data

Mercer, James L.
  Managing urban government services.

  Includes bibliographical references and index.
  1. Municipal government—United States.
2. Municipal finance—United States. 3. Municipal
services—United States—Finance. I. Woolston,
Susan W. II. Donaldson, William V. III. Title.
JS341.M47   352'.0072'0973   81-66228
ISBN 0-8144-5725-8   AACR2

First Printing

TO

William H. Carper, City Manager (retired) of Raleigh, North Carolina, a career professional who gave me the opportunity to practice public administration and tell others about it, and to Warren Jake Wicker, Assistant Director, Institute of Government, University of North Carolina at Chapel Hill, who taught me by example what it means to be a true professional.

JAMES L. MERCER

My parents, Frances and Banning Whittington.

SUSAN W. WOOLSTON

Edward Maruska, Director of the Cincinnati Zoo, a friend who showed me a way to be twenty-eight again at fifty.

WILLIAM V. DONALDSON

PREFACE

THIS BOOK is an outgrowth of the experiences of three people in public sector management. The discussions leading to our writing this book began and culminated during a series of seminars on "Managing with Reduced Revenues" that we were involved in at the University of Michigan.

This book is intended to introduce administrators and managers to some ideas, techniques, and tools that will be useful in the decade of the eighties. It can also be used by professors and students of public administration and political science as classroom or outside reading material and case studies.

Our original conception in writing this book was to look at strategies local government managers can use when faced with reduced local resources that result, for example, from local taxpayer revolts and inflation. But with the advent of the Reagan administration, this book is particularly timely, because it addresses such issues as increased local responsibility and managing well with modest resources.

There is no doubt that the new administration's belief that many programs can be carried out more effectively and efficiently at the state and local government levels than at the federal level will result in pressures for better management at these levels of government. Local administrators will need to find the best ways to evaluate their programs, to set priorities, and to cut back with the least suffering. Local managers will need more than ever to share experiences of successful service delivery realignment and budget trimming such as we present in this book.

The Reagan administration's philosophy and plans for the federal government will have massive effects on local management. Federal aid will be reduced substantially, ending programs such as public service jobs and sewer construction grants. Managers will have to guide their communities through this period of withdrawal of high levels of federal financial aid.

With less federal aid, new sources of local and state revenue will be needed. This book addresses alternative revenue sources as well as alternative and joint funding arrangements to deliver services more efficiently.

The new administration seeks to have fewer federal regulations. This will have positive effects in freeing up resources, but it may also put more pressure on local managers and elected officials to make complex, technical decisions. For example, local officials will need the tools to be able to evaluate when energy and economic development can proceed compatibly with environmental protection.

This book emphasizes practical ways local managers can meet the challenges of a new decade in which local governments will have increased flexibility to design programs and allocate resources without conforming to uniform national patterns. This book deals with local self-sufficiency, with ways to collaborate with the private sector, and, above all, with ways to serve citizens better at the least cost.

We would like to express particular appreciation to Dr. Charles Levine, University of Maryland, who worked with us in conducting the Michigan seminars. In addition, we wish to thank those who have written about some of the current topics of the day whom we have quoted or paraphrased and therefore footnoted as references in our book. We would also like to thank our families for their patience and understanding while we were working on the manuscript.

Specific thanks and appreciation are expressed to Mrs. Carolyn Lawler, who very conscientiously typed most of the manuscript, and to Alice Tippett and Shirley Novak, who assisted. Thanks, too, to our editors at AMACOM for their expeditious and excellent efforts.

We would also like to recognize and pay tribute to the dedicated public officials who daily work to bring better government to the citizens of this and other countries.

JAMES L. MERCER
SUSAN W. WOOLSTON
WILLIAM V. DONALDSON

CONTENTS

MANAGING
URBAN GOVERNMENT
SERVICES

1

ENTERING THE ERA OF
REVENUE REDUCTION:
TEN TRENDS TO WATCH

IN THE 1980s, local government administrators will face circumstances of constraint wholly different from conditions they operated under during the past two decades. The sixties was the decade of federal largesse, with consequent expanding revenues, responsibilities, and opportunities for local governments. The seventies appear in early retrospect to have been a transitional decade, when the very real problems of inflation, energy, and public cynicism began to constrain local government resources. Expectations about what government might accomplish not only stopped growing; to some extent, they reversed themselves. Citizens began to perceive government negatively—as part of the problem.

We must now look ahead and try to understand what the 1980s hold in store. What are some of the trends and pressures that will influence urban strategies for the 1980s? Here are ten that local administrators need to be aware of. They highlight much of the material discussed in detail in later chapters.

1. *The conflict between energy supply and development and environmental protection will intensify.*

As a result of programs carried out in the 1970s, substantial progress has been made in water and air quality improvement. The energy crisis threatens this momentum and may even reverse it. Environmentalists will let this occur only after extensive media, legislative, and legal battles. Local administrators will be caught up in this turmoil. A recent manifestation of this conflict is the new national interest in synthetic fuels. Their development will cause more air pollution, scar the landscape, and exacerbate regional hostilities. In addition, by the mid-1980s, the coal industry is expected to grow at an annual rate of about 5 percent per year. Coal will be used more because of high oil prices, uncertainty over natural gas supplies, and the political problems of nuclear power. Coal, too, creates many environmental problems. Another example is the practice of many motorists of putting leaded gasoline in their cars, thereby making their catalytic converters useless.

Problems of energy shortages and conservation will affect almost all local government activities, from improving fleet management to conducting energy audits to developing community energy management plans. With regard to land use, local governments will have to evaluate the economic and energy consequences of new development to determine whether it can pay its own way. Local governments will begin to look at encouraging growth in and around declining center cities and close-in suburbs. Such economic development plans may make the attainment of federal clean air standards more difficult.

Finally, local government caught in "energy booms" with massive influx of people and industry will need a great deal of assistance. Service delivery, housing, and the protection of environment and farmland will all be crucial issues.

2. *The urban financial crisis will continue.*

Neither Cleveland nor New York has yet proved that a city can recover successfully from the brink of financial disaster. Many cities live on borrowed time. Recession, inflation, municipal bond market problems, and taxpayer frustration with government all spell more, not less, financial distress for cities in the 1980s.

New York's deficit of more than $450 million can be remedied only if the city can be more successful in negotiations with city unions, if federal and state aid are increased dramatically, if costs can be controlled in education, health, and hospitals, and if the local economy remains fairly strong. It is unlikely any of these optimistic ifs will come true.

City accounting practices must be improved so that managers can clearly see what revenues are coming in, what is being spent, and how wide the gap is between them. The public in the next decade will demand such information. Cash accounting does not allow for sound financial planning. It does not provide any basis on which to project what labor negotiation decisions arrived at today will actually cost in future years and whether future revenues will permit these obligations to be met without further borrowing. Another problem is municipal pension fund accounting. Few cities even know what future costs will be, let alone whether revenues will be adequate to pay pensions owed to today's employees. City financial management is also hampered by the existence of many disparate funds, a lack of attention to the depreciation issue, and inadequately managed transfusions of federal and state funds.

At a minimum in the 1980s, the responsible local administrator will need to make sure that an accurate and updatable picture of the local government's finances exists and that financial procedures conform to guidelines of the Municipal Finance Officers' Association (MFOA). Disclosure to the public of a true picture of a city or county's condition as soon as possible may make citizens more understanding when times get harder and the budget-cutting choices become more limited and more painful.

3. *The post-World War II "baby boom" population will reach middle age; the impacts on cities will be dramatic.*

In 30 years, the proportion of the elderly in United States society will have increased substantially. This plus the increase in working women, declining birth rate, and decrease in the number of traditional family households all signal that changes will be needed in public services and facilities. Recreation and health services, for example, will take precedence over law enforcement as the teen-age population declines. Private companies are already planning to meet these trends; government should do the same.

In the second half of the 1980s, fewer people will be entering schools and colleges, but the demand of middle-aged working men and women for adult education, both career-related and non-career-related, may redirect usage of such facilities. Increasing leisure and high education levels of working adults in the 1980s may combine with longer lives and less mobility because of fuel prices to radically enhance the role of community colleges. They may become increasingly the providers of nearby, relatively inexpensive enrichment courses, ranging from physical fitness to languages to a rekindling of interest in the time-consuming arts and crafts of earlier decades.

4. *In the 1980s, the water crisis will be widely recognized.*

Water is being wasted and polluted at an alarming and increasing rate. More than 600 billion gallons a day are consumed in the United States today, compared with about 40 billion gallons in 1900. In some places, underground sources are being depleted so fast that the land is sinking. The big users of water are large-scale agriculture and industry, the latter mostly in cooling processes. Domestic uses such as home plumbing and yard care consume only about 9 percent of the water used daily. Nevertheless, these activities are being carried out with little interest in conservation because water is underpriced. The parallel with the use of oil in previous decades is obvious.

Water problems for the 1980s and beyond include water rights, energy development (synthetic fuels production requires massive amounts of water), pollution and treatment, regional shortages, and the quality of drinking water.

Governments will need to inventory water supplies. Measures to stop waste should focus on innovative agricultural practices that conserve water. Technology is available for water recycling, but there is little demand for these systems. Local governments should consider whether municipal water charges reflect the finiteness and potential scarcity of the resource.

Because most every plan to increase the water supply in one city or region would result in a decrease in some other city or region, intergovernmental negotiation and cooperation will be crucial when the water crisis arrives. The enormous growth of Southern California could not have happened without Colorado's water. Phoenix is blooming in a desert because of borrowed water. What will happen when the givers have no more to give? A 1977 drought cost farmers in the Southeast and in California billions of dollars. In 1979 drought caused similar difficulties in the Southwest.

While there is a need for national attention to this issue, the answer is not a new Department of Water in Washington, eager to regulate, ration, misallocate, and pontificate. The lead should be taken locally.

5. *Infrastructure maintenance will be a principal focus of city activities.*

As the Committee on Future Horizons of the International City Management Association (ICMA) has concluded:

> The continual, and expensive, maintenance of water and sewer lines, bridges, power plants, utility connections must continue. Deferred costs of maintenance, repair and replacement are simply additions to the mortgages of the future.[1]

Infrastructure maintenance will be ever harder because of cutbacks in federal and state aid. Managers increasingly will have to develop accurate, inexpensive ways of assessing regularly the conditions of streets, traffic lights, bridges, and other such facilities. The most efficient repair schedules should be developed; strategies such as recycling asphalt and buying longer-lasting street striping materials should be employed.

6. *Local government activities will have more international aspects.*

Urban management efforts in states such as California, Texas, and Florida have been affected for decades by the pres-

---

[1] "New Worlds of Service II—Local Government Strategies." Excerpts from the Report of the International City Management Association's Committee on Future Horizons, October 1979. *National Civic Review,* February 1980, p. 73.

ence of illegal aliens. Similar problems are now occurring in cities, counties, and towns in various parts of the country where Southeast Asian and Cuban refugees are being resettled. As the economy worsens and competition for jobs intensifies, resulting conflicts will add to the burdens of local governments.

A different type of international impact involves the increasing interest of foreign companies in investing in the United States. This is attributed to the fluctuating status of the U.S. dollar, the size and attractiveness of the American market, and this country's apparent political stability.

The competition for foreign plant locations will increase in the coming decade. Some 25 states have economic development offices in Europe and more than ten have offices in Japan. The skills of people charged with attracting foreign investment are quite different from traditional local or state administrative skills. Cities can work with states to enhance the "package" for overseas investors.

Availability of energy and transportation, quality of labor, the nearness of markets and suppliers, and tax incentives are the criteria for foreign investment decisions. The Japanese Sony Corporation of America built a $50 million, 800-employee factory in Dothan, Alabama, because it was geographically convenient for its South American markets, because it wanted to get away from California's taxes, and because it was enthusiastically welcomed by city and state officials. The Michelin Tire Company of France has recently opened an 1,800-employee plant in Dothan. In the last decade, South Carolina has attracted over $3 billion in foreign investment, making cities such as Spartanburg and Greenville high-growth areas.

Promotional advertising by local and state governments might seem incongruous in an era of cutback but in reality may reflect sound strategy with major long-term payoffs. The U.S. Department of Housing and Urban Development (HUD) has recommended that coordination of incentive programs for foreign investments is a promising federal strategy to assist distressed urban areas in the next decade.

7. *The need for productivity improvement through the introduction of new technologies and innovative management techniques will become more acute.*

In the 1980s, it is likely that the federal government will encourage local governments to initiate or increase productivity programs. Local governments can make more and better use of new scientific and technological products and processes and save money and improve operations as a result.

The National Science Foundation's National Innovation Network, consisting of regional innovation groups and three national technology-sharing networks all designed to assist local governments to innovate, has been successful. One of its best features is its commitment to follow the agendas of local governments that seek technological or technical assistance, not to intervene with predetermined state or federal mission objectives to see if these might incidentally coincide with what the local people are worried about or trying to accomplish. The National Innovation Network experiment to help local governments innovate deserves as much national attention as has been paid to recent federal efforts to encourage industries to become more innovative.

8. *Automation and advances in information technology will dramatically affect local government operations.*

In the 1980s, almost all large local governments (over 50,000 population) will use a computer to carry out some functions. Typical uses are record keeping, calculating, and payroll. More sophisticated applications will use computers to develop optimal routes for refuse collection or snow removal equipment, locate new public facilities, develop air quality models, and project land use patterns.

Local government office operations will become automated to a much greater extent. New technologies will be used in local government offices to control high labor intensiveness and rising costs of operations. Alternatives to paper creation, reproduction, and storage, such as the use of microforms or magnetic storage, will come into much greater use. New technologies such as advances in electronic data processing, word processing, reprographics, teleconferencing, and teleprocessing will become commonplace. The impacts of these technologies on people in the work environment will come under much greater scrutiny, and administrators will need to attend to the technical and social aspects of information and automation technologies.

9. *Citizen and media pressures will increase for areawide service delivery.*

The costs of the balkanization of government will be more widely recognized. Proposition 13 and its progeny show that citizens are closely examining all facets of government, beginning at the local and state levels. There will be hard questioning of the costs of proliferating special districts, as well as the duplication resulting from several small towns or cities providing similar services in a relatively small geographic area.

Traditional citizen resistance to areawide service delivery may erode when inflation and cutbacks dictate that a service can be provided only on an areawide basis or not at all. Annexation laws may be liberalized or proposed in states where they do not now exist. City/county consolidation proposals will reappear. At a minimum, local government should experiment with interlocal contracting and pooling of equipment and personnel, when appropriate.

10. *Transportation problems in the 1980s will increase in complexity and difficulty.*

Transportation and land use are closely intertwined. Local officials control land use decisions; many transportation decisions, however, are made by the states and the federal government. This and the energy crisis will make more difficult solving the urban transportation problem in the 1980s.

Automobiles, which epitomize in consumer goods the bedrock American belief in individual freedom and mobility, are not going to go away. Technology will eventually make them operable without gasoline. The nation's highways will continue to need maintenance. It is likely that more people will try to live closer to their offices; public policies should make this as easy as possible.

Local government officials should recognize the future role of the automobile but also consider other possibilities. For example, aeronautical technology advances will make possible a new generation of cleaner, quieter, safer, fuel-efficient commuter aircraft and helicopters. Such aircraft have a potential role in taking the pressure off overcrowded hub airports, expanding the use of secondary airports in less urbanized areas (a prospect with major economic development effects), and reducing congestion in ground-based urban transportation modes. Although these aircraft won't be available until near the end of this century, urban policy makers and planners should take these possibilities into account in planning and land use decisions. Secondary airports, for example, should not be closed but should be considered as possible key elements in regional development strategies.

In transportation, as in so many other public sector activities, good solutions are interjurisdictional, and funding is almost always intergovernmental. Not only do public administrators have to evaluate technical and social (efficiency/equity) merits of their decisions but they have to recognize that multigovernment coordination may be equally important or even override other aspects in determining the success of strategies chosen. Developing this ability to recognize that the intergovernmental element may determine whether specific local functional responsibilities can be carried out successfully may be the true challenge of the 1980s.

WHAT THIS BOOK INCLUDES

This book is drawn from the authors' experiences in many public administration environments. In the preparation of this book, the incorporation of those experiences was supplemented by research and a thorough review of the current public sector literature.

Chapter 2, "Organizing for the Eighties," provides an

overview of the traditional forms of local government organization, traces the various organizational structures of project or matrix management, describes the mature matrix form of local government organization, and discusses some of the traits of an effective matrix manager. The matrix organizational stucture is expected to be used by a greater number of local governments during the 1980s.

Chapter 3, "Alternative Revenue Sources," describes and discusses a variety of alternatives to the property tax that local governments might adopt to raise or maintain revenues during the decade ahead. It also considers the advantages and disadvantages of other tax sources and services for a fee.

Chapter 4, "New Fiscal Strategies," discusses the fact that in an era of reduced revenues and cutback management, local governments must reassess their fiscal strategies and financial management practices. It offers clear-cut guidelines for local administrators to use in developing an integrated and sound approach to budgeting, accounting, financial reporting and auditing, and debt management.

Chapter 5 is entitled "Interjurisdictional Financing and Service Delivery." It discusses various local government financing and service delivery strategies such as pooling of equipment or resources, interlocal agreements and contracting among jurisdictions, annexation, and governmental consolidation.

Chapter 6 is a case history of what management strategies were used in Cincinnati, Ohio, during a time of reduced revenues. It provides numerous helpful suggestions that can be of value to other local governments.

Chapter 7, "Improving Productivity," describes a number of techniques and strategies that can be used by a local government to improve productivity during the next decade. These include reorganizing services, increasing employee motivation, employing new technologies, and improving work standards, measurement, and scheduling.

The title of Chapter 8 is "Using New Technologies." It describes new hardware, software, systems, and other technology tools that help local government administrators reduce costs, increase productivity, and avoid future costs.

In an era characterized by rising costs and shrinking revenues, which the eighties are predicted to be, it becomes increasingly important to establish and rank funding and cutback priorities. The purpose of Chapter 9, "Establishing Priorities," is to suggest effective ways this can be done. It presents, in a practical way, three techniques for establishing local government priorities: Nominal Group Technique, Delphi technique, and Interpretive Structural Modeling.

Chapter 10, "Personnel and Personnel Management," discusses the new skills that local government managers and staff need to acquire to manage more effectively during the eighties. It also describes specific approaches that can be taken to strengthen the local government personnel function.

Local governments are turning increasingly to the private sector for assistance and joint ventures in all aspects of operations. Chapter 11, "Collaborative Strategies with the Private Sector," discusses this area of increasing interdependence. The private sector has shown great interest in public/private collaborative efforts. This chapter covers three areas of those efforts: voluntary, joint business ventures, and privatization.

The subject of Chapter 12 is "Intergovernmental Relations," a growing and changing area of local government involvement. This chapter gives considerable insight into how local governments can operate more effectively in intergovernmental relationships.

Chapter 13, entitled "Energy, Environment, and Land Use," points out that the 1980s will be characterized by a continuing energy dilemma and that the environment will probably be of secondary importance on the national policy agenda. In addition, local governments will continue to experiment with innovative strategies for managing both growth and population decline. This chapter deals with the intricacies and trade-offs among the issues of energy, environment, and land use.

Chapter 14 "Strategies for Change in Local Government,"

discusses many practical elements of how positive change is developed and implemented in a local government setting. One of the co-authors, on the basis of substantial local government experiences, gives helpful insights as to ways to introduce change and to gain its acceptance.

Chapter 15, "Toward the Year 2000," suggests some of the conditions and forces—political, economic, and social—that will affect local governments in the 1990s and beyond. It considers implications for today's managers and administrators.

2

ORGANIZING FOR THE EIGHTIES

EARLY IN THIS DECADE of the eighties America's cities and counties are caught up in a web of cost increases, revenue reductions, and extraordinarily complex decision making. The reasons have been amply addressed in recent public sector literature relating to the phenomenon of California's Proposition 13 and the resultant trend to "cutback management." Basically, they result from increased costs brought about by

Shortages, such as energy.
Double-digit inflation.
Higher labor rates.
Higher construction and materials costs.
More complicated decision making resulting from citizen participation.
High labor intensity and low productivity of the workforce.

On the other hand, revenues are the same or less because

Citizens are tired of paying more property and other taxes.
Citizens are resistant to paying higher service charges.
Residential and industrial tax bases are moving out of central cities.
Bond issues are difficult to pass.

How can local governments organize themselves to deal more effectively with these problems in the decade ahead and to lay a solid foundation in order to address new and more difficult challenges that they will undoubtedly face as they approach the year 2000?

Although traditional approaches have been adequate in the past, it is quite conceivable that new circumstances and demands in the 1980s may call for different types of organizational structure. This chapter will discuss some options that are available to local government management and will analyze the subtleties and intricacies of personnel relationships that may exist within these new organizational structures.

FIRST-GENERATION ORGANIZATION

The first-generation organization is characterized by a pyramid. It has been used extensively throughout history to fight battles, rule kingdoms, operate churches, manage businesses, and manage cities and counties as well. This type of organization is also referred to as the "traditional form of organization." It embodies a unity of command from the top down. There is a single leader or "boss" at the top of the pyramid. Authority is delegated downward through the organization to subordinates for the performance of those activities that lead to accomplishing the organization's objectives. Ultimately all persons in the organization are responsible to the chief executive, although there may be intermediate managers and supervisors who possess delegated authority from the chief executive over their own groups of subordinates.

In classical management concepts, the manager's authority was based on his legal rights. Usually, the manager was the founder or owner of the organization or enterprise. His right to command was inherent in these ownership rights. All orders flowed downward from a central authority, the manager, in a rigid chain of command. In this early form of organization, there were few opportunities or provisions for charismatic leadership, for horizontal lines of authority, or for authority based on expertise and interpersonal skills. It was virtually inconceivable that any manager would have to divide resources with another manager, negotiate priorities for his

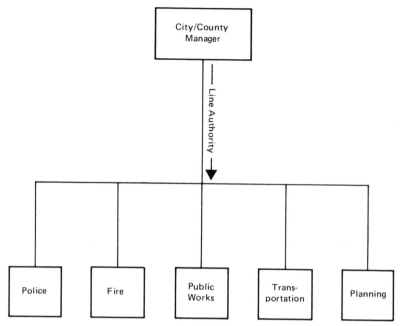

Figure 1. The traditional first-generation local government organization.

budget and other resources, or motivate others to act instead of simply "commanding" others to do his bidding.[1]

In local government, this conventional type of organization has often been manifested in a city or county manager or elected or appointed chief executive officer at the top of the pyramid with a number of functional department heads reporting to him (see Figure 1). Line authority for carrying out assigned activities or functions is delegated downward vertically through the organization. Some form of this pyramidal organization is still in wide use today by a majority of local governments across America. It is quite adequate for carrying out traditional local government activities, but it doesn't provide for cross-functional activities or projects.

[1] "Project Management: Past, Present and Future: An Editorial Summary." *IEEE Transactions in Management,* August 1979, p. 49.

SECOND-GENERATION ORGANIZATION

The second-generation organization is characterized primarily by an overlay of project or program managers or coordinators on the traditional pyramid organization. Their assignments may be temporary or permanent and usually result in a horizontal cross-cutting of the vertical lines of authority that are characteristic in the first-generation organization. Although probably used in some form throughout history (such as a king's emissary dispatched to "coordinate" a treaty proposal), this project overlay type of organization was formalized and attained significant stature in the post-World War II era, primarily in the aerospace and defense industries. It became fashionable during the 1950s in the Polaris Missile and space programs of the U.S. Department of Defense (DOD) and the National Aeronautics and Space Administration (NASA).

These new missile and aerospace systems were so intricate and complex and their timing so critical that the classical or pyramidal model of organization proved inadequate for managing them. It was difficult, if not impossible, to hold one individual responsible for the development of such complex systems. During this period, the manager was confronted with the coordination and integration of vast resources—human, material, and technical.

In addition, the coordination of a large number of outside contractors was crucial to the overall success of the effort. Many different activities and functions, such as research, engineering, testing, production, and support, had to be interwoven throughout the life of the project in order to produce a successful end result. Great demands, therefore, were placed on the military/industrial manager. The job was to coordinate a diverse group of activities and disciplines over a long period of time. This person might have been called a "multidisciplinary manager," except that such a phrase is unwieldy.

The task of getting these complex systems built and delivered cut across the usual organizational or pyramidal lines. Functional boundaries within management organizations had to be violated. Somehow an organization had to be developed that blended the traditional structure with technical knowledge among diverse disciplines. The first-generation or pyramidal organization was just not up to the test.[2] The solution, of course, was *project management.*

PROJECT MANAGEMENT

In the private sector and in the public sector at the federal level, project management has evolved as a recognized discipline with its own terminology, tools, procedures, and responsibilities. Project management has not been as common in state and local governments, but its use is expected to increase dramatically during the 1980s to deal with the added complexity of providing services to local government constituencies.

Project management has been used in industry in various forms under such names as project control, project coordination, project engineering, and liaison engineering. Basically, the concept provides a single point of responsibility for a project, exercises centralized control over information, and permits contribution to the project effort from functional organizational elements on a decentralized basis.[3]

Projects may be defined as activities that require the integration of efforts or services from several diverse disciplines or sources or require specialized attention because of their delicacy or importance. Projects usually have distinct life spans from inception to operational start-up. They may be performed totally "in house," they may be "contracted out," or they may be a combination of the two. Examples of typical local government projects include:

Planning projects for new public facilities, such as a fire station.

A *study project* of alternative service delivery mechanisms.

Internal projects, such as development and implementation of a new management information system.

---

[2] "Project Management: Past, Present and Future," *loc. cit.*
[3] Charles H. Marks, "Managing Industrial Projects." *Automation,* February 1969, p. 70.

Contract projects, such as design and construction of a new sewage treatment plant.

Continuing projects, such as street maintenance (if emphasis is required to play "catch-up.").

Projects costing several thousand to several million dollars.

Under most conditions, the use of the project management concept should no longer be necessary once a project reaches its operational stage. At that stage, the need for close coordination of diverse groups and elements should no longer be required, and control of the activity can shift to the appropriate line or functional manager (for example, the operation of a newly built fire station shifts from a construction project manager to the fire department).

The tools employed by project managers include Gantt and Milestone Charts, Program Evaluation and Review Technique (PERT), Critical Path Method (CPM), Line-of-Balance (LOB) Technique, and other networking approaches. Project review meetings, visual display techniques, monitoring of project progress, and exception reporting techniques are also tools used by project managers.

Essentially, project management may take four forms in the second generation. These are (1) staff coordination, (2) project office, (3) project-oriented matrix, and (4) functional-oriented matrix. Many local governments will have used one or more of these forms of project management organization, which are described in the following sections.

Staff coordination

In the first of the second-generation forms of project management organization, one or several persons are assigned to positions as staff coordinators for specific projects. These individuals usually report to a manager (for example, city or county manager) who has authority over most or all functional or other resource elements that will be involved in accomplishing the project. The staff or project coordinator interacts with the various functional element (contributing department) members and cuts horizontally across the pyramidal organization.

The project team thus consists of the coordinator, or leader, and various functionally assigned members (Figure 2).

The project coordinator sometimes works directly with the manager of a contributing functional department who, in turn,

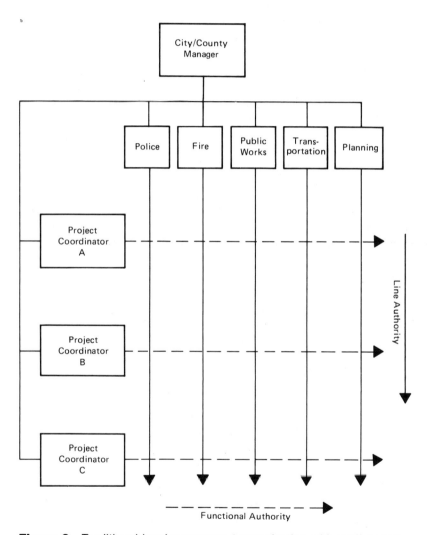

Figure 2. Traditional local government organization with staff coordination function temporarily added.

delegates the required work within his or her own organization. Under this arrangement, the functionally assigned members are not wholly committed to a project. The carrying out of the project assignment is accomplished by virtue of the project co-ordinator's ability to bring together diverse functional elements and resources. The only authority is implied by the reporting relationship to the chief executive officer. There is no direct line authority over functional department specialists who must contribute to the project. The project coordinator is, in effect, a staff manager. Hence, the term *coordination* rather than *management*. For success to be achieved in this second-generation project coordination environment, the coordinator assigned must be an unusual individual with special traits and approaches to the task. (More on this subject will be discussed later.) Under this project coordination arrangement, the potentially disrupting effect on the existing line or pyramid organization is minimal.

Other evolutions of this second-generation local government organization provide for project managers overlaid on the traditional pyramid organization. Three forms that this organizational arrangement may take are the project office, the project-oriented matrix, or the functional-oriented matrix.[4] In all these organizational arrangements, the project manager has considerably more actual authority for carrying out other responsibilities than does the project coordinator, previously described. These three forms of project organization are now discussed separately.

Project office

Under the project office arrangement, one or more project offices are set up at the same time the more traditional functional organization is maintained in place. All team members report to a project manager, who may be an assistant city or county manager or who may hold another general management title. No other functional departments, such as police, fire, or public works, are involved. All contributions from within the city or

[4] Marks, *loc. cit.*

county (internal) are contracted for by the project office. Similarly, all contributions from outside firms or vendors (external) are on a contract basis. Contracts, both internally and externally, may be selected by competitive bid.

This type of project organization is almost analogous to establishing a separate function, perhaps with a limited life, to manage a major effort, but it usually uses the tools of project management. Such a project organization might be used for the construction of a major capital improvement, such as a new sewage treatment plant. The majority of the design and construction work would be contracted for from outside firms, but there might be special emphasis placed on the project internally to ensure that costs and schedules are being monitored. A diagram of the organizational relationship of a project office is shown in Figure 3.

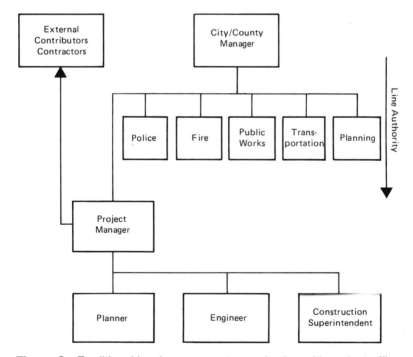

Figure 3. Traditional local government organization with project office added.

Project-oriented matrix

Under a project-oriented matrix arrangement, team members from various existing functional departments are assigned to a project manager for the duration of the project. The project manager usually reports to a general-management-level person, such as a city or county manager. An example of its use might be in the design and construction of a number of mini-parks, to be accomplished primarily with in-house resources. The project manager would be appointed by the city or county manager or an assistant. Each functional manager in the organization who would be involved in the project would assign an individual to the project manager for the duration of the project. Thus, the Parks and Recreation Director, the Chief Engineer, the Public Works Director, and other department heads to be involved would assign an individual to the project manager. Other needed resources, such as those of the city or county attorney or real estate department, might be contracted-for only on an as-needed basis. Under the project-oriented matrix, the project manager assigns, supervises, and integrates the work of the project team members. Functional department heads support their assigned project team members with technical know-how, training, and provisions for continuity of staffing, hiring, promotions, and salary. The project manager is responsible for project direction and control. He or she controls the *how, what,* and *when* of the project. This organizational arrangement is shown in Figure 4.

Functional-oriented matrix

Under the functional-oriented matrix, a project manager is appointed by a general-management-level person. The project manager interacts directly with the contributing functional department members who have been assigned to the project. The project manager cuts horizontally across the vertical lines of authority of the functional department manager. The project team consists of a leader, the project manager, and team members representing various functional departments. The team is

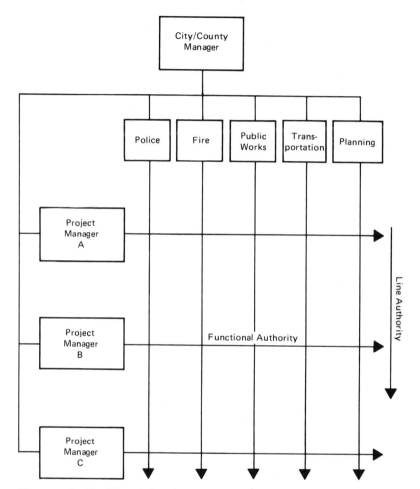

Figure 4. Traditional local government organization with project-oriented matrix added.

not wholly committed to the project, however, as it was in the two previous examples. The team must work within an organizational matrix of project versus line. As will be discussed later, it is not a mature matrix form of organization in which project members clearly have two bosses.

The individual project team members retain their primary

reporting relationships to their functional department supervisors, who are responsible for their technical performance and support, training, professional growth, salary, and so forth. The functional department supervisors control the *how*. The project manager controls the *what* and *when*. The major effort of the project manager is to integrate the team members' performance into the overall project objective. This can be accomplished by use of the manager's clearly defined position, persuasion, broad knowledge, and occasionally, if conflicts arise, by general agreement with the functional department head and the city or county manager. The project manager has responsibility for project direction.[5] A diagram of this type of project organization is provided as Figure 5.

Success in the functional-oriented matrix requires an unusually disciplined and technically well-qualified project manager. Widely used in the private sector, this form of project management has come into greater use in recent years in the public sector as organizations have become more complex. More on the unique type of individual that this type of project organization requires will be discussed later.

Thus far, the discussion has covered the staff or project coordination function and has described three types of project organizations that may be applicable for local government. The next section describes the mature matrix, or the third-generation local government organization.

THE THIRD-GENERATION LOCAL GOVERNMENT ORGANIZATION

The third-generation local government organization has evolved over the past two decades through the project organizational stages previously described. It is referred to as a mature matrix. It violates all the rules of one person, one boss. The success of this type of organization depends upon a particularly effective top executive and unusual people in project and functional roles within the matrix organization. In this third-gen-

5 Marks, *op. cit.*, pp. 70–71.

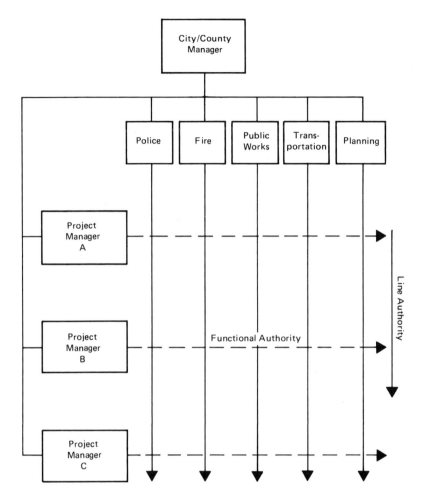

Figure 5. Traditional local government organization with functional-oriented matrix added.

eration local government organization, the project manager clearly has two or more bosses.[6]

The mature matrix imposes a dual-authority relationship over the project manager. Power is balanced and shared

[6] Stanley M. Davis and Paul R. Lawrence, *Matrix*. Reading, Mass.: Addison-Wesley, 1977, pp. 40–45.

equally between at least two bosses, each representing a different dimension of the local government organization (for example, public works and special programs). Both managers share
in creating an environment in which the project manager can
succeed. Their own success depends on how well they cooperate
to achieve positive results. A diagram of the mature matrix organization is shown in Figure 6.

Applying the matrix

An example of a project manager's typical assignment in a mature matrix organization might be for development of an ongoing formal training program in the use of new equipment in
the Public Works Department. Both of the project manager's
"bosses," the Public Works Director and the Manager of Spe-

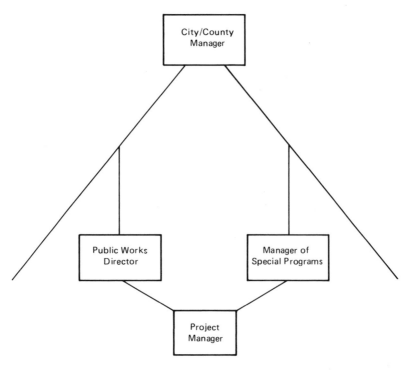

Figure 6. The third-generation local government organization: the mature matrix.

cial Programs, will be evaluated equally by the City/County Manager as to whether the project is carried out effectively and within a time schedule. Therefore, they each share in the desire to create a climate in which the project manager can succeed.

In this example, someone outside the Public Works Department is needed to assure the proper attention, time, effort, and consistency that such a training program requires. The Public Works Director does not have the necessary resources or the overall city or county perspective. The project manager has the perspective and many of the resources. However, a successful training program in public works cannot be carried out without the full support and enabling authority of the Public Works Director.

The city or county manager establishes a mature matrix organization to accomplish the desired objective. In this case, the city or county manager directs the Manager of Special Programs to appoint a project manager to be responsible for developing a training program. It is made clear to all concerned at the outset that the project manager will have the necessary authority to carry out his assignment and that he must satisfy two bosses, the Manager of Special Programs and the Public Works Director.

A mature matrix project management approach is being used by a few private sector organizations, but, to the authors' knowledge, it is not being used in any local government organization. However, with the increasing sophistication of managing, it is likely that more mature matrixes will be in use in the next decade in both the private and public sectors.

What works best?

Of the several types of project management and matrix organizations described, what works best? That, of course, depends on what is to be accomplished. In many situations, the traditional functional organization is best. That's why it has lasted so long. In others, a special need may be met by the mature matrix. In most situations, the best approach probably lies somewhere in between.

The *staff or project coordinator* may be effective in certain circumstances, but this individual lacks authority to direct activities within the project environment. He or she must be effective by sheer force of personality and by getting others to work together toward a common objective on the basis of the "reasonableness" of the effort. This is at best an impotent form of project organization. If you have a delicately balanced functional organization, it could, however, be the least threatening to the line functional manager.

The *project office* can be effective, but it basically establishes another functional entity that is concerned with completing a major project. It is not widely applicable because it is the type of organization that lends itself to large, complex projects, such as the construction of a new sewage treatment plant.

Some form of *matrix management* organization may be best. Although the various forms of matrix management seem to violate the one-boss rule of conventional management, both the private and public sectors are increasingly turning to matrix organization. This form of organization integrates today's complex requirements while maintaining the basic traditional organization but also focuses appropriate emphasis on activities and items of special need.

One of the biggest problems in introducing any new organizational scheme is overcoming resistance to change. Most people within the organization fail to recognize the new and increasing demands being placed on managers. Managers and subordinates at first feel uncomfortable in a new, loosely defined matrix organization. However, over time the barriers to change have begun eroding and now evidence is accumulating of the positive results that a matrix type of project organization can produce.

The *project-oriented matrix* can be very effective in producing results, but it has a jolting effect on the traditional organization. Much of the technical and managerial portions of the project work are transferred from the line functional departments to the control of the project manager. Functional team members have to be uprooted from their present organizations and placed under the direction of a new boss. Even if this doesn't involve a physical move, their traditional relationships are disturbed. It also raises questions about where the team member "returns to" in a functional department once the project is completed.[7] Many career path questions are raised by this form of matrix organization.

The *functional-oriented matrix* has less of a collision-type impact on the existing functional organization. The responsibilities and duties of the line departments don't basically change. The functional departments continue to provide technical expertise related to the project while the project manager provides the management. This is in direct contrast to the project-oriented matrix previously mentioned and is usually more palatable to the line functional managers.

Even though the functional-oriented matrix provides for less centralized control by the project manager, it provides a practical framework for integrating intricate and complex projects. The project manager and his or her team most often stay together for the duration of the project, but if the project doesn't place full-time demands on team members, they have time to work on other projects or on functional efforts in their line departments. Their career paths are clearer and are not disrupted as much as they are by the project-oriented matrix or the project office form of organization.

Even though each team member, in effect, has two bosses, it is not as formalized as in the mature matrix. When the project is large enough that functional team members can be assigned full-time for extended periods of time, the opportunity for conflict between the project and functional line managers is lessened. When team members are assigned to several projects at the same time or when functional duties in their home department keep them occupied part of the time, conflict may arise. Marks lists three rules to adopt to minimize such conflicts:[8]

1. When possible, plan work on a full-time basis for a short period of time rather than share work over a longer period of time.

[7] Marks, *loc. cit.*
[8] Marks, *op. cit.,* p. 72.

2. When time-sharing is required, plan for a fixed schedule over a fixed period of time (that is, 20 hours over a week's period of time).
3. Establish at the outset that conflicts which may arise should be resolved by the assistant city or county manager or some other designated general management person.

The *mature matrix* represents a total splitting of the project manager's relationships with two bosses. As long as the pendulum swings rather evenly between the two, few conflicts are likely to arise. Problems occur when one boss starts making greater use of the project manager than the other or when one boss is stronger than the other. The general-manager-level person to whom the bosses of the project manager report must create a climate for success in such relationships. This is a most sophisticated type of organizational arrangement. Care should be exercised in its use unless the flexibility exists to do a bit of experimenting.

CHARACTERISTICS OF A MATRIX MANAGER

As has been mentioned several times, a special kind of individual is needed to perform well in a matrix or project management environment. What are some of the important characteristics of such an individual? A matrix or project manager must be

A superior leader.
Technically knowledgeable about the project being managed.
Able to integrate the activities and efforts of diverse groups and individuals.
Knowledgeable about the organization within which he or she works; what it will, can, and will not do.
Experienced with a proven track record of accomplishments that has gained the respect of peers, managers, and subordinates.
A dynamic and persuasive personality.
A hard worker, fair, and able to motivate others.

Able to juggle resources to get the job done within time and cost constraints.

Flexible enough to handle changed directions and respond positively.

Able to exercise good judgment at all times.

A good planner and possess a good business sense.

Knowledgeable about the tools of project management and about when and how they should be applied.

Able to deal with all types of people and situations and keep a level head.

Good at expressing ideas, both verbally and in writing.

Able to resolve interdepartmental conflicts.

All forms of matrix or project management are potential areas for conflict. The line or functional team members have a primary loyalty to their own manager and department. The project manager is in direct competition for each line manager's resources, budgets, and prerogatives. Since the project manager has no formal authority over the functional managers, his biggest problem is gaining the support of these other managers for the project goal. This is accomplished largely by knowledge and persuasion. The basis of authority is fragile and must be supported by top management's presence and participation. It must be made known that cooperation is expected at all levels for the good of the organization. The project manager's authority will be enhanced when he or she is accorded the same status as other managers, as evidenced by office space, involvement in policy decisions, and participation in key staff meetings.[9]

THE FUTURE OF MATRIX MANAGEMENT

Project or matrix management is becoming widely used in the private sector. Its use in the public sector is expected to increase dramatically during the decade ahead as managerial requirements increase in complexity. The key to success in applying

[9] "Project Management: Past, Present and Future," *op. cit.*, p. 50.

matrix management is to select a diplomatic but forceful individual who can gain the respect of line and staff managers alike.

SELECTED READINGS ON MATRIX AND PROJECT MANAGEMENT

Ansoff, H.I., and R.G. Brandenburg, "A Language for Organization Design: Parts I and II." *Management Science,* August 1971, pp. B–705–731.

Argyris, Chris, "Today's Problems with Tomorrow's Organizations." *Journal of Management Studies,* February 1967, pp. 31–35.

Auerbach, I.L., "Changing from Hierarchy to Matrix." *Innovation,* March 1972, pp. 22–29.

Butler, Arthur G., "Project Management: A Study in Organizational Conflict." *Academy of Management Journal,* March 1973, pp. 84–101.

Cleland, David I., and William R. King, *Systems Analysis and Project Management.* New York: McGraw-Hill, 1968.

Davis, S., "Building More Effective Teams." *Innovation,* October 1970, pp. 32–41.

Davis, Stanley M., "Two Models of Organization: Unity of Command Versus Balance of Power." *Sloan Management Review,* Fall 1974, pp. 29–40.

Davis, Stanley M., and Paul R. Lawrence, *Matrix.* Reading, Mass.: Addison-Wesley, 1977.

Delbecq, Andre L., Fremont A. Shull, Alan C. Filey, and Andrew J. Grimes, "Matrix Organization: A Conceptual Guide to Organizational Variation." Wisconsin Business Papers No. 2, Madison, Wisc.: University of Wisconsin Bureau of Business Research and Service, September 1969.

Gailbraith, Jay R., "Matrix Organization Design." *Business Horizons,* February 1971, pp. 29–40.

Goggin, William C., "How the Multidimensional Structure Works at Dow Corning." *Harvard Business Review,* January–February 1974, pp. 54–65.

Grinnell, Sherman K., and Howard P. Apple, "When Two Bosses Are Better Than One." *Machine Design,* January 9, 1975, pp. 84–87.

Kay, Emanuel, *The Crisis in Middle Management.* New York: AMACOM, 1974, pp. 137–141.

Kingdom, Donald Ralph, *Matrix Organization: Managing Information Technologies.* London: Tavistock, 1973.

Levin, Richard I., and Charles A. Kirkpatrick, *Planning and Control with PERT/CPM.* New York: McGraw-Hill, 1966.

Part of this list was taken from Stanley M. Davis and Paul R. Lawrence, *op. cit.,* pp. 233–235.

Likert, Rensis, "Improving Cost Performance with Cross-Functional Teams." *Conference Board Record*, September 1975, pp. 51–59.

Likert, Rensis, and Jane Gibson Likert, *New Ways of Managing Conflict.* New York: McGraw-Hill, 1976.

Marquis, Donald G., "A Project Team + PERT = Success or Does It?" *Innovation*, May 1969, pp. 26–33.

Mee, John F., "Ideational Items: Matrix Organization." *Business Horizons*, Summer 1964, pp. 70–72.

Mercer, James L., "Local Government Organizational Structures for the Eighties." *Management Information Service Report*, International City Management Association, March 1980, pp. 1–12.

Mercer, James L., and Edwin Koester, *Public Management Systems.* New York: AMACOM, 1978.

Peters, Thomas J., "Beyond the Matrix Organization." *Business Horizons*, October 1979.

Sayles, Leonard R., "Matrix Management: The Structure with a Future." *Organizational Dynamics*, Autumn 1976, pp. 2–17.

Sayles, Leonard R., and Margaret K. Chandler, *Managing Large Systems: Organizations for the Future.* New York: Harper & Row, 1971.

Shull, Fremont A., Andre L. Delbecq, and L.L. Cummings, *Organizational Decision Making.* New York: McGraw-Hill, 1970, pp. 187–208.

Smith, Robert A., "The Matrix Organization Form: A Social Concept for Enterprise Effectiveness." National Aeronautics and Space Administration, George C. Marshall Space Flight Center, Management Development Office, November 15, 1966.

Wiest, Jerome D., and Frederick K. Levv, *A Management Guide to PERT/CPM.* Englewood Cliffs, N.J.: Prentice-Hall, 1969.

3

ALTERNATIVE REVENUE SOURCES

CALIFORNIA'S Proposition 13 and its backlash across the country, although not as severe as some people feared, will make increased revenues much more difficult to obtain in the 1980s. Local governments will need to seek new fiscal approaches and strategies. They will have to upgrade and streamline their financial management practices to stretch the revenues they can obtain as far as possible.

The purpose of this chapter is to explore and describe some alternative sources of revenue that local governments can develop. The next chapter will include a discussion of strategies for improved financial management including budgeting, accounting, and debt service.

What actions can local governments take to find alternative revenue sources at a time when their traditional source of revenue, the property tax, is being severely challenged? The answer probably lies in creatively combining alternative revenue sources, including new forms of taxation, user fees, and state assistance.

The most obvious alternative fiscal strategy for a government facing revenue reduction is to seek new sources of revenue to supplement what has been lost. The first step is to review special enabling legislation and constitutional limitations on the local government's ability to raise money. This includes taxing powers, debt limitations, bond authorities, and special assessments.

Alternative revenue sources need to be evaluated in terms of their *efficiency* and *equity* impacts. By efficiency is meant the best allocation of resources from an economic standpoint. For example, user charges tend to allocate resources more efficiently because they provide accurate information about demand and will not lead to over- or underproduction of a public good. On the negative side, they tend to exclude low-income persons from various city services and programs.

The equity criterion refers to the distribution of wealth. How much attention is paid to this criterion is dependent on public officials' value judgments concerning the role of government in redistributing income.

Taxation is the power of public officials to exact compulsory payments from citizens for the purpose of raising revenue. Sources of tax revenue include land, people, businesses, and human activities, such as the purchase of food and goods, the transfer of wealth from one generation to the next, and leisure pursuits such as fishing. Proposed tax alternatives should be evaluated systematically by public officials to determine which are most appropriate to meet a local government's and its citizens' goals. Criteria for tax evaluation include:

Yield. How much money can be raised.

Incidence. Who will bear the actual tax burden.

Elasticity. Percent change in revenue source depends on percent changes in incomes, price levels, population, inflation, or other factors.

Impact on markets. How it will affect the demand for housing, for example, in various areas.

Implementation costs and effects. How much it will cost to administer or enforce.

Legality. Legal constraints imposed by the state, for example.

Citizen acceptance. More difficult in light of Proposition 13; anticipate which groups will oppose for political or philosophical reasons.

Avoidance. How easily it can be avoided.

Four categories of alternative revenue sources will be discussed in detail in this chapter. They are other taxes, user charges or fees, state assistance, and federal and miscellaneous sources.

OTHER TAXES

Real estate or property taxes have traditionally been the principal source of local government revenue. The property tax was the focus of citizen dissatisfaction expressed in Proposition 13. In November 1978, voters in Idaho and Nevada rolled back property taxes to one percent of market value. Alabama approved an amendment to the state constitution that lowered assessments on most real property. Missouri passed a measure authorizing the state legislature to lower the property tax. While similar measures were defeated in some states, there is no doubt that renewed efforts in coming years to reduce property taxes will affect local governments.

The most logical step to replacing the property tax as a major source of local government revenue is through substitution of alternative taxes. Assuming state enabling legislation permits, several possibilities exist.

Local income tax. A local income tax provides additional revenues without increasing the property tax. Currently, only about one-fifth of the states allow local jurisdictions to levy such a tax, and only four states give counties this authority. In the 1980s, it is likely that more jurisdictions will be granted this authority. In terms of equity, the local income tax is progressive, because it increases as income increases. Cities can tax the income earned in their jurisdictions by nonresidents. This tax is usually administered locally, and the costs of administration are fixed. Withholding methods reduce direct taxpayer involvement.

Sales tax. If levied broadly, the sales tax may generate large revenues at low rates with diffused payments. This tax has been the primary producer of state revenues during the past decade. Its use by local governments is steadily increasing, with about 20 percent currently using it as a local option. The sales tax is a highly regressive tax that can be made more equitable by excluding essentials, such as food and medicine. Also, inclusion of both goods and services in the category of items to be taxed improves its equity. The tax extends to nonresidents and is relatively easy to administer. Because this tax automatically adjusts to changes in prices, it is sensitive to variations in economic conditions.

Hotel/motel tax. A hotel/motel tax could be a particularly lucrative source of local government revenue in resort or convention areas. The convention business is expected to continue its extraordinary growth into the 1980s.

Local personal property tax. The personal property tax is a progressive tax because the more affluent members of the community pay the largest amount of tax. Automobiles are usually the base for this tax.

Commuter tax. A commuter tax is levied against people who live in one jurisdiction and commute into another to work each day. There would be some equity in this because commuters use the other jurisdiction's services and facilities while working and commuting. Toll booths might be used to collect this tax, but that raises other issues of legality. Usually, tolls are charged only to pay for capital improvements, such as highways or bridges. Also, there is some indication that commuters actually contribute more in sales taxes than they require in services.

Luxury tax. A luxury tax is levied on items such as boats and jewelry. These taxes can be difficult for local governments to administer and enforce.

Other taxes. Other taxes might include a shift from a flat rate to gross receipts on business and occupation taxes, or the institution of local government lotteries.

USER CHARGES OR FEES

In terms of equity, user charges or fees are paid by those who benefit directly from the service. Those who do not benefit do not have to pay. This method of revenue collection allows individuals living outside of a jurisdiction to share in the costs of certain of that jurisdiction's services.

In terms of administration, setting the proper rate or fee structure may involve considerable time and effort. Specific information about what the service actually costs the city or county must be obtained, as well as what it costs to deliver the service and collect the fee, for example, inspectors, gatekeepers, and the like.

In terms of responsiveness, user charges may lag far behind rising costs in times of continued inflation. User fees or charges have several unique characteristics.

- They may be used when specific beneficiaries of the service can be identified (that is, those who don't pay can be excluded from using the service).
- They regulate the quantity and quality of a government service to consumer demand.
- When substituted for taxes, user fees or charges reduce a local government's tax effort. This tax effort is a factor in calculating a local government's share of general revenue-sharing funds.
- User fees or charges are not deductible on an individual's personal income tax return; taxes are deductible.

During the last half of the 1970s, county governments increasingly turned to the user fee method of raising local revenues. In general, political resistance to user charges is high. Most citizens believe that they are already paying for government through their local taxes and don't like paying other fees.

One of the major impacts of California's Proposition 13 was "fee fever." Many local governments in California replaced reduced property taxes with new or increased fees for services. This was a viable alternative revenue source, but in some cases it was carried to extremes. Citizens became angry and started additional restrictive petitions against local governments' abilities to raise revenues through any method. Also, higher user fees or service charges may have definite negative effects on certain groups of people such as low- or fixed-income persons and first-time home buyers. Sliding scales that offer a reduced price or direct subsidies may counteract inequity. As long as good judgment and reasonableness are applied, user fees can be a supplemental or replacement form of local government revenue.

User fees and charges should be established on a basis similar to what a customer pays for a product or service in the private sector marketplace. Typical user fees may include such standard services as public hospital care, mass transit, water, and sewer use, and trash collection.

Some of the approaches that local governments can take to increase local revenues through user fees follow.

Parking rates. Parking rates at public lots should be consistent with what surrounding private parking lot owners are charging for spaces. The use of electronic flag droppers can add to collection. Fees can be imposed at public facilities such as convention centers, beaches, parks, and zoos. An appropriate trade-off must be struck between revenues to be obtained and the public's right of access to public facilities.

Tennis and golf fees. Fees for use of tennis courts and golf courses owned and operated by local government should be in line with what private courts and courses charge patrons.

Nonresident recreation use fee. Charge nonresidents, by card or per visit, to use public facilities such as parks, golf courses, and tennis courts.

Cost-based fees for special recreation programs. Charge for special recreation programs such as art and ceramics classes, teen clubs, leagues, and teams, on a cost or cost-plus fee basis.

Rent recreation facilities. Charge church and other groups to use public facilities for special events such as weddings, receptions, and dances. Also, investigate concession possibilities at all recreation areas.

Other services for a fee might include

Charges for police accident reports and fingerprint service.
Sanitation services on a full-cost basis.
Rental of police and fire personnel for special private functions.
Full-cost emergency ambulance fees.
Charge full cost for all reports provided to the public.
Charge full-cost marina and boat ramp fees.

Charge full-cost airport fees for fuel, tie-down, space and hangar rentals.

Rent special expertise and equipment to other jurisdictions (crime lab, lie detector, and so forth).

Charge full-cost for new recreational services such as dirt bike tracks, skateboard courses, bike and horse trails.

Charge full-cost animal control fees.

Light the golf course for night play and employ golf rangers to expedite play.

Institute double charges for utility customers outside the jurisdiction and review these fees for full-cost recovery.

Replace or repair slow-running or old water meters.

Impose street-sweeping charges.

Charge full-cost fees for residential and commercial inspections.[1]

In the wake of Proposition 13, several local governments in California developed some rather innovative fees and user charges. These included charges to high school students for summer school, admission charges to county museums and botanic gardens, full-cost fees to builders and developers, fees to repair cracks in sidewalks, and charges for fire safety inspections. One city even charged a fee to put out a fire.[2]

The trend toward raising local government revenues in the 1980s will be much more fee-oriented than ever before. The days of sole reliance on the property tax as a local government revenue generator are over.

STATE ASSISTANCE

During 1979, local taxes nationally increased by only 1.5 percent and property taxes actually declined by 2.9 percent. This

[1] Much of this section on fees and user charges was drawn from Charles A. Morrison, "Identifying Alternative Revenue Sources for Local Government," *Management Information Service Report*. Washington, D.C.: International City Management Association, July 1977.

[2] Stephen J. Sansweet, "Catch 13: Californians Discover Tax-Cut Mania Has a Corollary-Fee Fever." *The Wall Street Journal*, June 1, 1979.

was the smallest local government tax hike in five years and it is considered to be a direct result of Proposition 13. On the other hand, federal and state aid to cities and counties was $3.8 billion more in 1979 than it was in a similar period a year earlier.[3]

Throughout America's history, states have often played the role of regulator, supervisor, and provider of technical assistance to local governments in the area of financial management. Because of their legal authority over local governments, states can greatly influence and often can mandate the methods by which local government finances are recorded, reported, and verified, as well as how local revenues are raised, stored, and expended.

Because of the legal doctrine known as Dillon's Rule, states have legal superiority over local governments. In terms of local government finance, the state plays two roles:

1. A partnership function in which states work with local governments to reach common goals.
2. A problem-solving function where states become involved in local financial management to correct perceived deficiencies at the local level.[4]

Typically, local governments derive their powers to raise revenues from the states. Unless otherwise specified by home rule powers, the local government revenue bases and the tax rate maximum are specified by state law. In recent years, states have liberalized local governments' revenue-raising capabilities by the following methods:

• Enlargement of the local government property tax base by requiring frequent property reassessments and the use of more sophisticated real property reassessment techniques.
• By removing millage limits on property taxes.

[3] "Local Property Taxes Up Slightly in 1979, Property Taxes Fell, Tally Shows." *Washington Report,* June 30, 1980.
[4] John E. Peterson, C. Wayne Stallings, and Catherine Lavigne Spain, "State Roles in Local Government Financial Management: A Comparative Analysis." Government Finance Research Center, Municipal Finance Officers' Association, Washington, D.C., June 1979, p. ix.

- By permitting other local government tax sources than the property tax.
- By increasing state grants and financial transfers to local governments.
- By delivering public services directly.[5]

The state/local government revenue trends that will continue to evolve and gain greater stature during the 1980s are as follows:

Most states provide special revenue-raising authority to certain local governments, recognizing that they have special needs. These are usually the larger, more troubled local governments (for example, New York City). This will continue and increase during the 1980s.

Both state aid and local user fees and service charges are assuming a much more important and intensified role in local finances than are revenues from nonproperty taxes. This trend will accelerate during the 1980s.

As existing tax resources are exhausted, local governments are increasingly turning to the states for new revenues from taxes that states can levy, collect, and rebate to local governments without burdensome administrative requirements. This trend, too, will continue during the decade ahead.

Existing examples of the last item listed include the local option sales tax and the state motor fuels tax, which are collected by states, with a portion rebated to local governments. It appears that local governments prefer such aid to revenue-sharing or categorical grants from states.[6]

States can be asked to assume all special education costs. Schools can be financed through a state tax on a pooled industrial/commercial tax base, instead of by the regressive local property tax.

Local governments can also band together to seek more return of state revenues. For example, in Rhode Island, cities and towns asked to receive a percentage of the combined state

[5] *Op cit.,* p. 54.
[6] *Op. cit.,* pp. 55–56.

sales and income tax revenues. Tying municipal aid to these sources of revenue will ensure that as these taxes grow, so will aid received by local governments.

The 1980s will definitely see an increase in state aid to local governments and, with it, a concomitant increase in state control over local affairs. This is unfortunate because most people consider state government remote and far removed from their daily lives.

FEDERAL AND MISCELLANEOUS REVENUE SOURCES

Another major source of local government revenue is federal assistance from grants and revenue sharing. Other local government revenue sources include special assessment districts and packaging of revenue-raising measures early in the fiscal year in order to achieve maximum interest capability.

Federal grants

The average local government is by no means tapping all of the federal revenue sources that are potentially available to it. Possibilities to increase the knowledge about which grants are available may require the services of an outside grantsman or grantsmanship organization. If it does, the cost of this service can probably be justified in terms of the returns to the jurisdiction that will be obtained. The problem with a federal grant is that it may be one-time in nature or it may have strings attached that will cause a local government to give up local control. Even with such problems, federal grants will continue to be an important source of local government revenue during the 1980s.

Federal revenue sharing

During most of the seventies and into the early eighties, federal revenue sharing has been a substantial source of local government revenue. It has replaced many categorical grants that were previously available to local governments. The problem is that its continuation is dependent on politics at the federal, congressional, and executive levels. Those local governments that used revenue sharing funds only for special, one-time activities or capital improvements are in good shape, if funding is not renewed. Those that programmed such funds into their operating budgets would be in serious trouble if federal funding were stopped. Fortunately, it appears that federal revenue sharing will continue to be an important source of local government revenue well into the 1980s.

Assessment districts

The creation of assessment or urban service tax districts and the reevaluation on a true-cost basis of services within existing assesssment districts are other possible sources of revenue for local governments during the 1980s. Assuming the state enabling legislation exists or can be created, an assessment district is a defined geographic area where more services are demanded than the local government generally provides and where extra charges are levied for those services. In a county, an assessment district might be established for an area that is urban in character and requires urban services but for a variety of reasons is not in a position to be annexed to a city. Those services demanded of the assessment district above and beyond normal county services (twice-a-week sanitation collection or increased police and fire protection) would be paid for at a higher rate. Special assessment districts could also be created in existing cities or counties in specific geographic areas where higher than normal services are demanded (tennis courts for affluent neighborhoods or increased street maintenance in certain areas). In a sense, assessment districts are another means of imposing user fees in specific geographic areas.

Expand economic base

One of the best ways to increase local government revenues is through an increase in the number of business, industrial, and other organizations within the local community that pay taxes and user fees. Incentives to attract industry such as those described in Chapter 11, industry relocation campaigns, and other approaches will need to be taken by local governments during the next few years in order to stimulate greater local economic activity.

Better cash management

Professional management of a local government's idle cash and other funds is an excellent way to increase local revenues. Most local Certified Public Accounting firms can assist in this effort. They might suggest, for example, the use of computerized cash management systems that can lead to maximization of interest earned on idle cash.

Other sources

Other possible alternative revenue sources include

- Sale, lease, or rental of unused real and personal public property.
- In-lieu transfers from revenue-producing funds such as utilities (imposing administrative, management, or other charges on revenue-producing funds).
- Surpluses from discontinued funds.

4

NEW FISCAL STRATEGIES

IN AN ERA of reduced revenues and cutback management, local governments must reassess and reevaluate their fiscal strategies and their financial management practices. More stringent controls and practices will be required in the fiscal and financial areas of local governments in the decade ahead than in the history of local government financial administration.

DANGER SIGNALS

The president of the U.S. Chamber of Commerce, Richard Lesher, summed up the fiscal crisis facing America's local governments in this way:

> Fiscal distress in many of the nation's cities and other local governments is a priority public policy issue. Soaring costs for public services, a sharp decline in the economic base, outmigration of middle-income residents and other social problems have had a devastating effect on the fiscal condition of these municipalities. The result has been a serious deterioration in the quality of life and a decline in economic development and human productivity.[1]

[1] Richard L. Lesher, Foreword, *Improving Local Government Fiscal Management: Action Guidelines for Business Executives.* Washington, D.C.: Chamber of Commerce of the United States, 1979.

How do you know what the fiscal condition of your local government is at any given moment? One index is its cash solvency, or its ability to pay its bills or meet its obligations in the short run (30 to 60 days). A more comprehensive approach is to measure a local government's ability to pay all its costs of doing business. These include annually occurring and intermittent expenditure obligations such as capital items and preventive maintenance.[2]

In a situation where a local government incurs ever-increasing costs but has a declining revenue base, fiscal difficulty is inevitable. The government will not be able to meet its financial obligations in the long run. The Advisory Commission on Intergovernmental Relations has identified[3] several key danger signals that characterize a local government on the verge of financial difficulty. These are:

1. An imbalance in operating fund revenues versus expenditures, in which current expenditures significantly exceed current revenues during one fiscal period.
2. Consistent patterns over several years where current expenditures exceed current revenues by small amounts.
3. Current operating liabilities exceeding current assets.
4. Short-term debt in operating funds at the end of a fiscal year.
5. An increasingly high rate of delinquency in property tax payments.
6. A sudden decrease in assessed values for unexpected reasons.
7. A locally administered retirement system which is underfunded. *This may be one of the most serious and significant danger signs of all.*
8. Poor techniques for accounting, financial management, and reporting. These include:

[2] "Measuring Your City's Fiscal Condition." *Financial Management Digest,* National League of Cities, February 1980, p. 1.
[3] Advisory Commission on Intergovernmental Relations, *City Financial Emergencies: The Intergovernmental Dimension,* Washington, D.C.: U.S. GPO, July 1973, pp. 1–55.

- overestimating revenues and targeting expenditures to these overestimations
- using accounting practices that recognize revenues prematurely and that unnecessarily postpone expenses
- overestimating forthcoming state and federal aid so that more tax anticipation notes can be issued
- placing city-owned property on the tax rolls so that additional tax anticipation notes can be issued
- carrying forward receivables that are bogus
- assuming 100 percent of taxes will be collected
- applying pension fund earnings, in excess of the specified interest rate based on actuarial assumptions, to operating costs (even though the assumptions are out of date).

If these eight danger signals, or the local government fiscal practices that led to their use, go unchecked, a local government will likely get into fiscal difficulty. Short-term debt becomes a way of life and then, eventually, a local government finds itself unable to meet its long-term debt obligations

Other local government fiscal danger signals include a downgraded credit rating, significant outstanding litigation involving the local government, economic problems of a major local taxpayer, the unanticipated costs of a natural disaster, an increase in federal or state mandates without funds to cover them, and failure to adhere to generally accepted accounting principles in the local government's fiscal management.[4]

Most local governments are not in the conditions described here. Without sound financial management, however, they could be. The cost/revenue squeeze of the 1980s will force more and more local government fiscal defaults. As a result, more local governments may be tempted into using some of the unsound fiscal practices described.

How do local governments avoid or ameliorate financial problems in the 1980s? Their best avenue is through an inte-

---

[4] *Improving Local Government Fiscal Management, op. cit.,* p. 14.

grated and sound approach to budgeting, accounting, financial reporting, auditing, and debt management.

BUDGETING

Local government budgets are plans, but they are really much more. In a local government, a budget is a legally binding statement of anticipated revenues and authorized expenditures. Most states require that nearly all of a local government's principal fund types be budgeted (for example, Utility Fund). Even if it is not required, it makes sense from the standpoint of good financial management. Budgets may be either annual or long-term, operating or capital. The annual or current operating budget authorizes and controls revenues and expenditures for operations on a fiscal year basis. Some local governments prepare five-year operating budgets that project their revenues and expenditures well into the future. This gives them a better ability to project operating costs associated with new capital improvements coming on line in future years, and also sharpens revenue and expenditure estimating skills. Five-year operating budgets are excellent tools that can be used by local governments to good effect during times of rising costs and diminishing revenues. The use of this approach to budgeting should increase during the 1980s.

Long-term capital improvements budgets are usually prepared for a five-year period. These budgets include a variety of capital improvements, most of which extend over more than one year. Pay-as-you-go capital improvements, usually smaller projects that have a project period of less than one year, are often financed through the annual operating budget. Even when capital projects extend beyond one year, fiscal year closings are recommended so that a community's annual report is adequate and complete.

Almost all states require themselves and local governments to present a balanced budget. Any excess of expenditures over current revenues must be covered by borrowing.[5]

[5] *Op. cit.*, pp. 17–18.

Local government budgeting has passed through four basic periods. These are the:

Control period
Management period
Planning period
Cutback period

The control period generally covered the years 1910–1935. This was a time when the general public was disgusted by government corruption as epitomized by Tammany Hall and Boss Tweed. As a result, stronger controls were placed on the financial practices of local government. Emphasis was placed on

Line items/object accounts
Encumbrance accounting
Position control
Travel control

The next period through which local government budgeting passed was the management period, which lasted from about 1930 to 1955. This period resulted from the new interest in scientific management on the part of Frederick W. Taylor and others. During the management period of budgeting, emphasis was placed on

Efficiency
Output measurement
Performance measurement
Functional organization (the first step toward program budgeting)

Performance budgeting was the notable output of the management period.

The third stage through which local government budgeting passed was the planning period. This started in about 1955 and continues in some form today. It brought about a new kind of program budgeting, with more emphasis on planning, programming, and quantitative analysis. The major proponents of this type of budgeting included President Lyndon Johnson,

Secretary of Defense Robert McNamara, the Rand Corporation, and others. This period of budgeting resulted in PPBS, or Planning, Programming, Budgeting Systems, in which the master planning, program planning, and financial planning of an organization were fully integrated. PPBS placed more emphasis on the following:

Goal setting
Establishment of objectives
Effectiveness
Program structure crossing functional organizational lines
Program analysis (usually quantitative)

One of the major characteristics of PPBS was a program structure. Under this structure, local government programs such as public safety, public health, and transportation are listed at the top of vertical columns and the functional department expenditures for each program are listed at the left and are horizontally spread across each program. The advantage is that organizational budgeting emphasis is placed on programs, rather than on functions, objects, or line items as was true in previous budgeting systems. This provides the policy-making body with more meaningful information on which to base decisions about the number and level of various service programs.

Although the end result of PPBS—program budgeting *per se*—is in use by some local governments, its use today is not widespread. Because it is an excellent way to look at a broader picture of local government programs and their associated expenditures, interest in program budgeting will undoubtedly be rekindled during the 1980s.

The fourth period of budgeting might best be called the cutback period. It is charcterized by the use of zero-based budgeting (ZBB). Interest in ZBB became widespread about 1976 for two primary reasons. First, Jimmy Carter had instituted it when he was governor of Georgia. When he tried to implement it in the federal government, interest in ZBB spread to other state and local governments. Second, California's Proposition 13 forced local governments to consider using zero-based budgeting when determining cutbacks in service delivery. ZBB tracks the program budgeting process closely and prescribes a specific and detailed technique for priority setting. It also develops marginal costs of operation and places more reliance on bottom-up decision making about programs. Analysis is made of the efficiency and effectiveness of programs and the evaluation and prioritization of different levels of effort.[6]

In terms of budgeting systems, the 1980s will probably see many more local governments using program budgets. These budgets will incorporate some features of ZBB, probably attention to incremental costs and benefits, and the possibility of eliminating programs no longer needed, as well as some of the attributes of performance (efficiency) and line-item budgets (accountability).

Areas of budgetary concern that local governments must address during the coming decade include the following:

- Better ways of presenting budget proposals for review and approval, which discuss the fundamental purposes involved and the extent to which the budget proposals are expected to achieve certain public purposes.
- Budgets which reflect the full range of actual costs and effects of proposals (associated operating and capital costs, employee and associated benefits, and capital costs).
- Budgets which spell out future implications of proposals beyond the budget year.
- Budgets which present alternative courses of action and their associated costs and benefits.
- Budgets which reflect the fundamental purposes of proposed programs, what is expected to be achieved, and how such achievements are to be measured.[7]

Much greater depth of analysis needs to go into local government budgeting. The final output should be an easily understood product that reflects costs/benefits and implications of the chosen courses of action.

---

[6] *Op. cit.,* p. 21.
[7] Harry P. Hatry, "Strengthening the Budget Process." *Public Management,* August 1969, pp. 6–9.

ACCOUNTING, FINANCIAL REPORTING, AND AUDITING

A major public accounting firm recently concluded that in many local governments financial planning and budgeting are merely a series of clerical exercises conducted in a limited time frame.[8] There are two principal problems that hinder reforms of local government accounting and financial management systems.

1. Outmoded financial practices and procedures have frequently been more enduring than have local government administrators and elected officials.
2. Outdated provisions in city charters or state-mandated accounting and reporting systems prevent local governments from instituting sound procedures.

Although these barriers pose a hindrance, they do not preclude local governments from following budgeting, accounting, and reporting practices on the basis of generally accepted accounting principles (GAAP). Unfortunately, these principles seem to be honored in full by only a very few local governments.[9]

From an accounting and financial management standpoint, local government is a combination of several independent financial entities or funds with a self-balancing set of accounts. Each has its own balance sheet, operating statements, and, where appropriate, its own budget. Therefore, obtaining an accurate picture of the financial conditions of a local government as a whole is extremely difficult. If one wants to understand the overall financial condition of a local government, one must study the financial statements applicable to each fund and nonfund account group and, where appropriate, the associated budgets.

The vital connecting link between budgeting and financial reporting is the local government accounting system. The

---

[8] Arthur Anderson and Company, "Sound Financial Management in the Public Sector," Chicago, 1976.
[9] *Improving Local Government Fiscal Management, op. cit.,* p. 15.

budget establishes both revenue and expenditure levels, and, in so doing, it establishes the nature and scope of financial operations. The accounting system allows the summarization of results of financial operations. These can then be compared with budgeted amounts. If the actual amounts and the budget are not comparable, it is difficult to reconcile the differences. Adherence to minimum GAAP standards by local governments would prevent this problem.

Traditionally, the purpose of local government accounting and associated reporting systems has been to control the legal aspects of the revenue-expenditure process. In recent years, however, the systems have been used to a greater extent by local government administrators to manage more effectively. Within the past few years, more pressure has been put on local governments for fuller and clearer financial reporting. This has come from taxpayers, investors, independent auditors, securities analysts, and other governments. Demands for such reporting have often been engendered by local governments' failure to conform to the standards of GAAP. Of some 18,000 eligible local governments, only about 400 have fully complied.[10]

In a recent survey of 46 medium-size cities with populations ranging from 200,000 to 400,000, the accounting firm Coopers and Lybrand found the following problems of local government conformance with GAAP ground rules for external financial disclosure:

- 76 percent did not disclose the actuarially computed value of unfunded vested pension liabilities.
- 84 percent did not disclose the accrued cost of vacation and sick leave benefits.
- 26 percent did not and could not disclose the dollars invested in long-term assets.
- Of those that leased property, 93 percent did not disclose the lease arrangements or their associated future obligations.

[10]*Op. cit.*, p. 16.

- Of those having overlapping debt (such as school districts), most did not disclose the nature of those obligations.

- In terms of audits, contrary to recommendations of the National Council on Governmental Accounting, 41 percent did not have their books audited by independent CPA firms. In 70 percent of the cities that did, auditors took exception to the accounting practices.[11]

The haphazardness of local government auditing practices is one reason that revenue sharing has been criticized and challenged. The bottom line is that in the 1980s local governments should at least adhere to minimum GAAP standards in their accounting, reporting, and auditing practices. Adherence would help increase public and elected officials' confidence in information generated by the local government accounting system. It also will support investors' requirements for full and complete disclosure of the government's financial condition in bond-offering statements.

DEBT MANAGEMENT

Debt management refers to the governance of those decisions that control short- and long-term borrowing, the types of debt to be issued and their timing, and the design and sale of securities.

In general, local government officials should be aware of legal limits for the amount of long-term debt that can be issued, as well as the present position of indebtedness. Updating or adoption of an official debt limitation policy should be considered. Outside specialists should be used when issuing or administering debt.

As a percentage of the Gross National Product, local government debt amounted to 6.5 percent in 1949. Ten years later, it had risen to 10 percent, and it has remained at that level ever

[11] Coopers and Lybrand and the University of Michigan, "Financial Disclosure Practices of the American Cities," Philadelphia, 1976.

since. However, from 1949 to 1976, interest rates tripled. The effect of interest rate fluctuation since 1976 has been even more acute. Thus, the importance of managing debt during the 1980s is crucial to a well-managed local government.

However, at least two questions need to be answered: How much debt can a community afford? and What should it be used for? In general, long-term debt should not exceed $1,000 per capita, and debt service requirements should not be more than 20 percent of a local government's annual revenues. Also, preferably, debt should be structured in such a manner that 50 percent of it will be retired within ten years. Often overlooked is the overlapping debt on a local government by school districts, utility districts, and the like.[12]

There are two classifications of local government debt: general obligation and revenue debt. General obligation debt means that the full faith and credit of the local government stands behind the debt. The bondholder is assured that payment of principal and interest on the debt takes precedence over any other expenditures from the local government's tax base or that, if required, taxes will be increased to cover the debt. Revenue debt, on the other hand, means that the debt will be repaid from revenues derived from the particular project (such as a convention center where fees are paid for its use). Revenue bonds are generally less secure than general obligation bonds and therefore bear a higher interest rate. A new form of debt security that has come into use in recent years is the so-called "moral obligation debt." These bonds are revenue debt unless there is danger of default on payment. Then, the issuing local government may be obligated to repay the debt.[13]

Revenue debt may be of the following types:

- Revenue bonds issued to finance the construction, acquisition, or improvement of a facility where revenues are pledged to pay the debt.

---

[12] *Op. cit.,* p. 33.
[13] Irwin T. David, "How to Manage Long-Term Debt." *Urban Georgia,* May 1979, p. 19.

- Special assessment bonds, which are used to finance improvements pertaining to only one part of a community.
- Financing authority bonds, which might construct a local government facility to be rented by the local government.
- Industrial aid bonds, which are tax-exempt securities issued by local governments in order to attract industry.[14]

General obligation bonds and many revenue bonds are often used to raise funds for long-term capital improvements such as fire stations, parks, sewage treatment plants, streets, and so on. These are expenditures that are usually too large for the pay-as-you-go system.

One of the recent problems that has developed on the local government debt scene has been the difficulty of selling bonds at reasonable interest rates. Taxpayer revolts, competition, and soaring interest rates have caused some problems in the local government bond market. As a result, the cost of local government borrowing has never been higher.

A local government's debt capacity and ability to repay the debt are determined, to a great extent, by the collective opinion of financial analysts, underwriters, financial institutions, rating agencies, and the public. In order to convince these groups that new debt can be incurred at reasonable interest rates, local governments should provide

- General demographic information and other facts about the local government.
- Information about the structure of the local government and special-purpose units.
- Substantive data about the current bond issue.
- An overview of the local government's revenue and expenditure picture and other financial information.[15]

Local governments should also supply any other information that may be of value in the decision-making process.

---

[14] *Improving Local Government Fiscal Management, op. cit.,* p. 33.
[15] *Op. cit.,* p. 34.

OTHER FISCAL STRATEGIES

The International City Management Association has recently developed a system that can be used by local governments to anticipate fiscal and economic problems. It is a monitoring system that provides early warnings of possible financial problems. It also gives local government officials a better understanding of a local government's fiscal position.

It is not a particularly simple system, but it is workable. It identifies 13 factors that contribute to a local government's financial decline. In its broadest sense, the system enables a local government to answer three basic policy questions:

- Does the external environment provide the resources to pay for its demands on your financial situation?
- Do legislative policies and management practices enable responses to inevitable changes in the financial environment?
- Are your total operating costs currently being covered from a financial standpoint?

Answers to these questions will assist a local government in monitoring changes in its fiscal condition.[16]

---

[16] "Measuring Your City's Fiscal Condition," *op. cit.*, pp. 1–3.

5

INTERJURISDICTIONAL FINANCING
AND SERVICE DELIVERY

IN MOST STATES, municipal governments historically have
been the providers and deliverers of "hardware" services, such
as police, fire, public works, and utilities. County governments,
on the other hand, have been the providers and deliverers of
health, education, and welfare, or "soft" services. These traditional lines of differentiation have broken down during the decades of the 1960s and 1970s. The primary reasons for this
breakdown include urbanization of counties, demands by city
dwellers that their city government deliver both "hard" and
"soft" services, and the targeting of federal manpower and
other "soft" programs to cities. This initial targeting began in
the Great Society era of the sixties and expanded into other
areas of federal funding during the seventies.

In many urban areas, these trends have rendered obsolete
the existing arrangements governing the delivery of public services. Controversies concerning service duplication and inequi-
table financing arrangements can frequently be traced to the
inability or unwillingness of city and county governments to
implement the necessary structural reforms in their organizations or service delivery patterns.

Full consolidation of city and county governments, such as
the successful merger of Nashville and Davidson County, Tennessee, would appear to be one obvious answer to the problems

of service duplication or overlapping. However, during the seventies, there was vigorous opposition to most attempts at large-scale governmental consolidation and annexation in metropolitan areas. Such proposals encountered adverse reaction from both public officials and citizens. As a result, virtually all major service reorganizations that have been successfully implemented have been "piecemeal" transfers of individual functions, leaving intact the basic structure of the existing service delivery systems.

Citizen acceptance of governmental change is a difficult issue. It may be that taking the incremental approach today will enable larger issues to be tackled tomorrow. What are some of the strategies that local governments can pursue during the 1980s to deal with interjurisidictional financing and service delivery problems?

INTERJURISDICTIONAL STRATEGIES

Interjurisdictional financing and service delivery strategies include the following:

Pooling of equipment or resources among jurisdictions.
Interlocal agreements on service delivery or functions, or territories.
Interlocal contracting for services or functions among jurisdictions.
Alternative service delivery arrangements.
Annexation.
Governmental consolidation.

Pooling

Pooling is the concept of arranging with a neighboring jurisdiction to share or pool equipment or resources in order to accomplish a common objective. Such a concept might include arrangements between two or more cities, between a city and a county, among several counties, or a variety of other combinations.

Many cities have arranged with neighboring jurisdictions to loan fire, police, or communications equipment during emergencies, such as a tornado, flood, or a large downtown fire. However, because of the need in the 1980s for most cities and counties to manage with less resources, it is an appropriate time to consider pooling arrangements under nonemergency circumstances. Pooling arrangements can be formal written contracts or simply memoranda of understanding among jurisdictions. They might include a sharing or pooling of the following kinds of equipment, activities, or personnel:

- Large items of capital equipment such as road graders, leaf pick-up units, street pavers and sweepers, and specialized trash pick-up equipment. These would be high-cost items that are not used every day by an individual jurisdiction and can be shared when needed.
- Special experts such as a risk manager, planners, special police laboratory specialists, or a technology agent. This would be sharing of those specialties that are needed by both jurisdictions, but where the cost of one person or a special unit cannot be justified for each jurisdiction.
- Specialized items of equipment such as lie detectors, police and fire laboratory equipment, and instruments that are used only occasionally.
- Specialized facilities and talent such as those used for police and fire training; recruitment, selection, and testing of certain levels of personnel; crime laboratories; and specialized inspectors.
- Joint purchasing, data processing, and planning efforts to obtain greater economies of scale for both jurisdictions.
- Agreements to build a fire station, a sanitary landfill, or other such public facility, possibly on a common geographic boundary, and to share the costs and benefits of construction and operation on a 50–50 basis.

Pooling of fire-fighting personnel and equipment has produced substantial benefits for five small Illinois communities with populations ranging from 21,000 to 70,000 residents. Fire departments in three of the participating cities reported an annual combined savings of $675,000 in personnel expenses and $65,000 in equipment and maintenance costs.[1]

The communities—Arlington Heights, Buffalo Grove, Elk Grove Village, Mount Prospect, and Rolling Meadows—share manpower, equipment, and stations. The pooling arrangements expanded upon a mutual aid system that had been in existence for many years. The first pooling arrangement involved joint staffing of an ambulance by two cities. Each provided one person per shift. Three of the communities pooled their fire dispatching into one central facility, thus saving some $100,000 a year in salaries and equipment. Agreements for mutual manning and response allowed one rapidly growing community to forgo building a new fire station to meet its growing needs. This saved approximately $350,000.

The question of control has militated against joint efforts such as pooling in the past. Each jurisdiction must have appropriate access to the service or facility when needed. This must be assured in any pooling agreement. There can be legal barriers. Pooling appears to work best in communities that have a previous track record of cooperation.

Interlocal agreements

Interlocal agreements are negotiated among jurisdictions (city and county, several cities and a county, several cities, or several counties) to establish how governmental services will be delivered and financed within a prescribed area. An example of such an agreement is the provision of all water and sewer service by a city to a large area beyond its boundary, because the city's plants have the capacity, its personnel have the expertise, the source of water is the same, and the area is a natural drainage basin. Another example is a sanitary landfill operated by a county for itself and several municipalities. The idea is to agree on those functions and services that can best and most eco-

[1] John Hayden, "Pooling Firefighters, Trucks Saves Illinois Towns' Money." *Nation's Cities Weekly*, National League of Cities, March 19, 1979.

nomically be provided by each jurisdiction and on a plan to carry out such an agreement.

In 1979 a U.S. Department of Housing and Urban Development (HUD) study of four towns in Minnesota and their efforts to jointly administer various services concluded that joint agreements were effective for new services, those that had never before been provided, such as wastewater treatment, animal control, and garbage collection.[2] It was most difficult to obtain joint agreements in service areas where each town had already made a large investment and had a system in place with a strong sense of community identification, such as police and fire departments.

The interlocal agreement approach is likely to be fraught with politics and issues of self-interest, but definite efficiencies and economies of scale can be gained as a result of such agreements. In Muskegon County, Michigan, eight governmental units implemented, through an Interlocal Public Agency Agreement, a centralized police dispatching operation that resulted in cost savings, as well as service improvements.[3]

The problem solved by the centralized system included eight different law enforcement agencies operating independent, dissimilar dispatching systems in one 514-square-mile county. Three of the eight jurisdictions operated 24 hours a day, seven days a week. Other jurisdictions did not have trained dispatching personnel.

The first agreement entered into for centralized dispatching by these jurisdictions proved unworkable because small jurisdictions felt dominated by larger ones, since assessments and voting weights for the system were based on population. A second agreement creating the central operations for police services was signed in 1972 by eight agencies.

The centralized police dispatch operation in 1975 saved

[2] U.S. Department of Housing and Urban Development, Office of Policy Development and Research, *Practical Ideas on Ways for Governments to Work Together*, Washington, D.C.: U.S. GPO, May 1979.
[3] See Fred S. Knight, "Central Police Dispatch: A Realistic Goal." *Municipal Management Innovation Series*. Washington, D.C.: International City Management Association, December 1975.

about 42 percent in combined personnel costs to the participating agencies. Another benefit was increased cooperation on all facets of police work among officers of the different jurisdictions as a result of their using the same dispatching system. More police officers were freed for other duties since fewer were required for dispatching.

An ICMA evaluation of this interlocal service delivery agreement included among its findings:

> The Muskegon Centralized Police Dispatching System has demonstrated that police service efficiency and effectiveness can be improved as a result of multi-jurisdictional cooperation. . . . The issue of local autonomy and the responsibilities of locally elected officials to their constituencies must be given the highest priority in establishing any organization which depends on multi-jurisdictional cooperation.[4]

Other important aspects of this interlocal agreement were the county's role in ensuring coverage of unincorporated areas so that there were no gaps in the service delivery area, and the support of the chief administrative officers in the participating jurisdictions who championed this innovative effort and advocated its adoption to both elected officials and citizens.

Interlocal contracting

Interlocal contracting among local governments relative to services, functions, and geographic territories holds great promise for expansion in the 1980s. In a large metropolitan area, where there may exist one large city, ten or more smaller cities, and a combination urban/suburban county, it is unreasonable and uneconomical for a majority of them to furnish duplicate services. Granted, some functions such as police patrols may need to be provided locally by each jurisdiction in order to provide more emotional comfort to the citizens, but almost all functions and services could be provided on a larger scale, with various jurisdictions specializing in a particular function or service.

The basic concept is for City A to provide certain services, such as fire, police, public works, planning, and traffic engi-

[4] *Ibid.* p. 3.

neering, and to contract with City B to provide City A with such services as property appraisals, sanitary landfills, crime laboratories, and training facilities. City A might provide services one through ten; City B, services 11 through 20; and County A, services 21 through 27. Similar arrangements could be made according to functional groupings, such as public works, traffic engineering, police, and fire, or according to geographic boundaries. Such an approach could lead to greater specialization of labor and function and, therefore, to greater efficiencies and economies of scale. More movement in this direction will be seen during the 1980s, but because of local differences, politics, and local self-interests, a truly multijurisdictional, specialized service arrangement by function may never become a fact. That is unfortunate because such an approach holds great promise for increasing the efficiency and effectiveness with which local government services are delivered to citizens.

ALTERNATIVE SERVICE DELIVERY: A CASE STUDY

An approach to service delivery among many jurisdictions that encompasses some of the concepts of interlocal agreements and contracting but goes well beyond those is called *alternative service delivery.*

A recent initiative in Atlanta/Fulton County, Georgia, has taken this middle-of-the-road approach.[5] It has produced some potentially sweeping reforms. It went well beyond interlocal agreements and contracting but stopped short of the major surgery associated with metropolitan governmental consolidation or annexation. The Atlanta/Fulton County experience offers some valuable lessons in pragmatic reform within the constraints of big-city politics. The achievements of the blue-ribbon Atlanta/Fulton County Study Commission compare favorably with other recent governmental reform efforts in

[5] James L. Mercer and Allen L. White, "A Middle Road to Reform: The Atlanta/Fulton County Experience." *Western City,* January 1979, pp. 13–15 and 27.

Rochester, New York; Tampa, Florida; Portland, Oregon; and Denver, Colorado. The multiservice tax district proposal adopted by the commission is one of the most significant reforms in large-city government in the last decade.

Background

Citizens of Atlanta and Fulton County, Georgia, as in many metropolitan areas, have been concerned with local government reorganization for at least the past 25 years. The 1952 Plan of Improvement was intended to provide a permanent and rational reallocation of service responsibilities between city and county governments. The plan at once tripled the size of the City of Atlanta and permitted automatic future annexation of unincorporated county areas when they reached a prescribed level of urbanization. However, in 1969, a Georgia court ruled this provision unconstitutional, a decision which effectively terminated the opportunity for further territorial expansion of the City of Atlanta and paved the way for increased participation by Fulton County in the provision of municipal services.

As has happened in many counties surrounding large central cities, Fulton County by the mid-1970s had evolved into a full-service urban government, delivering most traditional municipal services to its residents in unincorporated areas. Since most such services are financed by the county's general fund, two-thirds of which is derived from Atlanta taxpayers, Atlanta citizens complained of fiscal inequity through double taxation. Fulton County responded with its own accusations of inequities because the county provided services at Grady Hospital in downtown Atlanta to a clientele comprised overwhelmingly of Atlanta residents. City, county, and state efforts in the early 1970s produced no viable resolution of these differences. By the end of 1976, it appeared likely that the rural-dominated Georgia General Assembly might impose a settlement. Governor George Busbee believed that continued city/county friction posed a major threat to the passage of other legislation proposed by his administration. These conditions set the stage for a concerted effort to resolve the problem.

The Atlanta/Fulton County Study Commission

In March 1977, Governor Busbee appointed the Atlanta/Fulton County Study Commission, a group of 19 persons representing business, civic, and governmental interests at the local and state levels. Former Federal District Court Judge Sidney O. Smith was appointed as chairman, and Dr. Tobe Johnson of Morehouse College was appointed vice-chairman. Busbee charged the commissioners to undertake a thorough and objective analysis of the delivery of governmental services and associated revenues of Fulton County and its municipalities, including the City of Atlanta, to ensure that all citizens receive adequate services at an equitable cost.

In May 1977, the commission appointed a small staff and accepted a proposal from a team of researchers from Battelle Southern Corporation and Public Research and Management, Inc. The eight-month research agenda consisted of three major components:

1. Description of the present governmental service delivery system.
2. Analysis of current and projected problems in the existing system.
3. Design and evaluation of an alternative service delivery system.

At one of its first meetings, the commission identified the key issues to be considered in the study:

1. Questions of service delivery and cost inequities.
2. Financing public hospital and health services.
3. Public housing.
4. Social services.
5. Tax assessment and collection practices.

The commission also decided to hold two sets of public hearings; one at the start of the study to gain citizen input on service delivery and financing problems, and a second set at the conclusion of the study to report on the commission's work and recommendations. It also decided that each public service should be studied separately, without constraints imposed by a predetermined model delivery system.

Working papers and memoranda were prepared by the researchers and distributed to the appropriate working committees. These papers described the existing service delivery arrangements, their financing, and their major strengths and weaknesses. The committees reviewed the papers, requested supplementary information, and used them as a basis to evaluate alternative service delivery options and financing schemes. These efforts were supplemented by interviews with local officials, comparative budget analyses, and an analysis of the crucial "subsidy issue." After completing the service-by-service analyses, the committees brought specific recommendations to the full commission for discussion and action. After adoption by the full commission, draft legislation was prepared for each recommendation and eventually submitted by the governor to the Georgia General Assembly.

During the eight-month study, the full commission met 13 times, and each of the three committees met at least nine times. The high level of sustained interest and participation by the commissioners reflected the importance placed on the study by the governor and the public; it was widely perceived to be the last real opportunity for many years for local determination of the extent and nature of governmental reform in Atlanta/Fulton County.

The commission's final recommendations for change are shown in the list on the following page. Of the 26 services studied in detail by the committees and reviewed by the full commission, 13 received recommendations for change. In some instances, the recommendations had few, if any, immediate cost impacts. These, not unexpectedly, encountered little resistance to passage.

A second group of recommendations called for greater involvement by the state in financing the services. After resolving questions of feasibility, these recommendations received quick approval by the commission.

A third group of recommendations urged or mandated

Recommendations of the Atlanta/Fulton County
Study Commission

Service	*Key Recommendation*
General Government	
Code Enforcement	Mandate uniform codes.
Elections	Clarification of office qualifications.
Planning/Zoning	Increased coordination across jurisdictions.
Tax Assessment/Collection	Revise qualifications of assessor and appeals process.
Physical/Environmental	
Libraries	Transfer entirely to county.
Solid Waste	Transfer disposal to county.
Traffic Engineering	City contract to other jurisdictions.
Water and Sewer	Merge city/county systems.
Public Protection/Health/Welfare	
Adult Probation	State assume greater financial role.
Emergency Medical Services	Support for integrated statewide system.
Hospitals	State assumption of a portion of the costs of the major regional hospital.
Fire Service	Create fire districts throughout county.
Recreation	Support increased city/county cooperation.
Financing	Create tax service districts for all area-specific services.
Annexation	Prohibit without consent of the annexed population.

Services studied for which no change was recommended by the commission included:

Business Licensing	Electricity/Gas	Courts
Data Processing	Street Lighting/Cleaning	Police
Public Housing	Coroner/Medical Examiner	Public Health
Agricultural Services	Corrections/Jails	Social Services
Aviation		

greater city/county coordination and cooperation. No functions were actually transferred, and fiscal impacts were negligible. This group of recommendations also received quick approval by the commission.

A fourth group of recommendations presented the greatest
challenge for the commission. These recommendations would
have direct impacts on allocation of service responsibility
and/or financing:

- County assumption of library and solid waste disposal
  functions.
- Expansion of a fire district concept already existing in two
  unincorporated areas to all the remaining unincorporated
  areas of the county. This shifted fiscal responsibility to
  those direct recipients of the service. Accompanying this
  was a recommendation for centralization of fire training
  and investigation.
- Eventual merger of city and county water and sewer systems and equalization of rates charged to all customers. A
  nine-member board would be created to oversee the development of a comprehensive, long-range plan for the distribution of new water lines. Disputes would be arbitrated by
  a majority of the active judges of the Superior Court of
  Fulton County. This recommendation encountered considerable opposition from the county because of its investment in plant and equipment, but it eventually passed the
  full commission.
- Expansion of tax service districts to include all those services whose recipients are area-specific. This was the most
  hotly contested of all of the commission's recommendations. In a final compromise, the commission agreed to tie
  the tax service district recommendation to a companion
  recommendation that would effectively eliminate the possibility of future annexation of unincorporated areas by
  the City of Atlanta. Also included was a phase-in period of
  five years to help offset the expected 9 to 13 mill tax increase that would impact incorporated areas. Overall, this

was viewed as a major step forward in resolving the long-standing "subsidy" debate.

A last service, police, is especially noteworthy because no change was recommended. Substantial research and debate concentrated on this activity. In the final decision, the demand for local control overwhelmed considerations of efficiency, effectiveness, and economies of scale. Despite the strong evidence in support of some centralization, such as in training, special investigations, and laboratory work, no strong advocate stepped forward to promote such changes. The result was a unanimous vote for "no change."

With the exception of education, the commission addressed all major services in the eleven jurisdictions within Fulton County. In some cases, it recommended changes in operation and finance: in others, it recommended the implementation of general principles to redress significant inequities and build the foundation for future changes. The commission operated for the most part at the general policy level; it did not have the time, resources, or the mandate to perform a series of management reviews or performance audits of individual operating departments in every government jurisdiction and seek to answer questions of broad significance to all citizens of Fulton County.

The commission's far-reaching recommendations relative to local service delivery won the early approval of the 1978 Georgia General Assembly and Governor George Busbee. Several recommendations required constitutional amendments and were placed on the ballot in November 1978. Because other legislation also required constitutional amendments, the ballot was extremely long and difficult to understand. The Atlanta/Fulton County recommendations narrowly passed in Fulton and DeKalb Counties, the two counties to be affected by the governmental changes. To everyone's surprise, the other counties in Georgia defeated the constitutional amendments related to Atlanta/Fulton County. This defeat was seen as a backlash from rural Georgia against the length and difficulty of the ballot.

Following the election, Mayor Maynard Jackson of Atlanta and Chairman Milton Farris of the Fulton County Commission met and agreed to implement as many of the recommendations as possible. It remains to be seen whether all the recommendations will be implemented and, if not, whether the Georgia General Assembly will take up the issue again at a future session.

Conclusions

The Atlanta/Fulton County experience points to the following conclusions:

- Proponents of metrowide governmental concepts will find support in neither core cities nor suburbs.
- Local control is the crucial concern to citizens in the services that most directly affect personal lives, such as police, fire, and zoning authority. Efficiency and effectiveness are secondary considerations in such instances, although they are key concerns in reorganizing other municipal services.
- Regardless of the value of the proposed changes and the top-level political support they receive, if they require a statewide vote, a backlash may occur if the ballot is too long or complex.

The experiences of the Atlanta/Fulton County Study Commission point to a middle road to reform that appears more palatable to all concerned parties than the more drastic options of large-scale consolidation and annexation. In spite of the difficulties expressed as to the statewide vote, much of the work of the commission is directly transferable to other cities and counties across the country that have similar fiscal inequities and organizational inefficiencies.

ANNEXATION

Annexation is the addition of territory to a municipality. It usually involves joining portions of territory that are unincorporated, less populous, and less developed to an incorporated, larger unit of government. Up until World War II, annexation had been the traditional way for a municipality to expand its boundaries and services. Most of the largest cities in the country were formed this way.

As suburbs surrounding metropolitan areas grow and become urban in character, they usually demand the same governmental services as are delivered to urban dwellers. In most cases, the core city they surround has a legal basis to annex the areas once certain provisions are met. Up until the past two decades, annexing of urban-like areas to the central city was one way of avoiding many of the service delivery and financing problems noted earlier in this chapter. However, as central cities began declining and as more affluent people moved to the suburbs, annexation has been made more difficult, if not impossible.

In order to be financially viable, the central cities need the tax base that has moved to the suburbs. The more affluent suburbanites fled the central cities because of higher taxes and crime and they do not want to be a part of the central city. They want either to live in the unincorporated county bordering the central city or to have a new incorporated area of their own. Since legislation relative to annexation usually requires an affirmative vote on the part of the citizens of the area to be annexed, virtual impasses usually occur. Affluent suburbs have grown to the point where they have a strong voice in the state legislatures, so difficulties in core city annexation of nearby suburbs are likely to continue.

Annexation has played a significant role in shaping the urban areas of today, but state statute restraints and the social differentials between cities and suburbs, which comprise the heart of the urban crisis, limit its future potential. Urban strategies for restructuring the relationships between cities and suburbs are unlikely to include annexation in the 1980s.

GOVERNMENTAL CONSOLIDATION

Governmental consolidation is the most comprehensive approach to the problem of efficient and effective interjurisdictional financing and service delivery. However, it requires such major change and is so fraught with politics and self-interest at all levels that it is difficult to accomplish.

The past two decades have witnessed some notable success stories in city/county consolidation. These have included Nashville-Davidson County, Tennessee; Jacksonville-Duval County, Florida; and Lexington-Fayette County, Kentucky. There have also been spectacular defeats of proposed mergers. These have included Charlotte-Mecklenburg County and Durham-Durham County, North Carolina; Sacramento-Sacramento County, California; Salt Lake City-Salt Lake County, Utah; and Tallahassee-Leon County, Florida, among others. At this writing, Louisville and Jefferson County, Kentucky, are planning to propose a consolidation, and Los Angeles-Los Angeles County, California, have appointed a committee to consider consolidation, among other options.

What have been some of the results of successful consolidation?

In Nashville-Davidson County, Tennessee, Former Mayor Beverley Briley says:

> People see that there's no buck passing now. There's only one legislative body and only one administrative division to carry out its orders.[6]

In Jacksonville-Duval County, Florida, Former Mayor Hans Tanzler states:

> Bankruptcy was avoided because merger lessened the incentive for people to move to the suburbs and increased government responsibility for the services provided.[7]

Of the Lexington-Fayette County, Kentucky, experience, Former Mayor H. Foster Pettit says:

> We found a change in the attitude of industry; companies don't want to come into a community where there are "fiefdoms" and political bickering.[8]

---

[6] Barbara Hadley, "Government Reorganization: Success Stories." Special Report, *Louisville Magazine,* January 1980, p. 34.
[7] *Ibid.*
[8] *Ibid.*

Louisville has had four unsuccessful attempts at governmental reform. Three of these took place during the decade of the seventies. Proponents of governmental reorganization in Louisville-Jefferson County argue that local residents are not being well served because of the many layers of government.

Jefferson County, Kentucky, currently contains 87 separate governments. These include county government, Louisville, and 85 smaller incorporated cities. In addition, there are more than 100 special local government entities, such as special districts and independent agencies.

Because of this proliferation of government, turf-guarding, suspicions, and confusion often create barriers to fruitful dialog among governments. Examples[9] include:

- The failure of county officials to request assistance from the city of Louisville's police department in 1976, when an unruly mob of antibusing demonstrators got out of control, although such aid was available.
- Lack of the Kentucky governor's endorsement in 1974 for a Louisville-area performing arts center, because city and county governments couldn't reach a consensus. This delayed the start of the Louisville cultural complex until 1979.
- Current inability of city and county to agree on a common cable TV supplier, delaying service to the community.
- Duplication of effort when economic development projects must deal with multiple governments.

Because of these problems, Louisville civic leaders point to the slow progress and the negative impact on civic pride that the present sitution has created.

---

[9] Charles Springer, "Government Reorganization: Help Wanted." Special Report, *Louisville Magazine,* January 1980, p. 24.

6

Case History:
MANAGING REVENUE REDUCTION
IN CINCINNATI CITY GOVERNMENT

CINCINNATI'S long history of professional city management and the civic dedication of its citizens have earned for the city a reputation as one of America's best-managed communities. It was this tradition of good management and civic concern that caused the city in the 1960s and early 1970s to expand its human service programs while maintaining the full complement of traditional municipal services. Even though the city's population and economic activity declined and a majority of its population were dependent citizens, Cincinnati continued to meet its citizens' needs. The city health program provided basic health care for its poorer citizens. Cincinnati's recreation programs were able to use one of America's best urban park systems to offer a variety of recreational opportunities. The police department pioneered team policing. The city continued to redevelop its downtown and organize its neighborhoods during a period when many cities were hard pressed to maintain basic services.

To finance both service expansions and maintenance of current service levels, the city's general fund more than doubled between 1964 and 1974. This increase in the general fund in the face of declining property tax revenues resulted from a local payroll tax and increased federal funds. Despite increases in the payroll tax in both 1970 and 1972, the income from the general fund did not keep pace with expenditure levels. Each year between 1970 and 1975, it became more difficult to balance the budget, and each year the options for balancing the budget became more limited. Acceleration in the collection of the payroll tax, reduction in capital spending, and elimination of some monies earmarked for maintaining the city's physical plant all provided one-time-only funds for balancing the budget. These strategies did not address the underlying problem of inadequate revenues to meet increasing costs.

Had the national economy been healthier in 1976, or had the city's general economic decline been reversed, the crisis of 1976–1977 might have been postponed for a few more years. The cumulative effect on the city's budget balancing devices combined with rising unemployment rates and inflation made a budget deficit in 1976 inevitable. If current levels of service were to be continued, projections indicated that by 1977 this deficit would increase to an unmanageable $16 million, even if salary levels could be contained at the 1976 level. The City Council faced the choice of either finding new sources of revenue or sharply curtailing its expenditures.

Because of the willingness of its citizens to support higher levels of payroll taxation in the past and the city's history of involving citizens in its decision-making process, a 0.35 percent increase in the payroll tax was proposed. The proposed tax increase was accompanied by an aggressive program of productivity improvement to reduce employment levels over the next five years. The tax increase and the productivity program were supported by both the Chamber of Commerce and the Central Labor Council. Most of the city's neighborhood organizations favored the increase and worked for its approval at the polls.

The tax proposal was endorsed by both major daily newspapers. There was no evidence of any organized opposition to the tax increase. Despite this overwhelming public support, the tax increase was narrowly defeated at the polls. The City Council had no alternative to reducing city expenditure levels in order to avoid an illegal budget deficit.

The steps the city administration initiated in 1976 to reduce general fund expenditures, with a minimum reduction in the level of services the city provided, would not have gained the acceptance and cooperation of the city's workforce if the City Council had not first tried to increase the city's income by a tax increase. The Cincinnati City Council's willingness to present a tax increase to the voters convinced the city employees that the fiscal crisis was real.

With the defeat of the tax increase proposal, the City Council directed the staff to develop a program for budget reductions including those that could be made at once. The staff asked for guidance in two areas: first, were the reductions to be temporary or were they to be based on a long-term reduction in city operating costs; and, second, what were the priorities for making the reductions?

It was determined that the long-term costs of deferring maintenance of capital facilities and of postponing replacement of capital equipment would result in staggering replacement costs in the future. The deferment of maintenance and capital replacement that had been used to help balance the budget in the last ten years had already jeopardized the city's capital facilities.

What seemed at the outset to be a relatively simple process of reducing the size of city government turned out to be almost impossible. One person's frills turned out to be another person's necessities. When examined for the long-range impact on the city and its redevelopment, reductions in support of cultural activities were seen to be poor economies. If the city's future health was dependent upon middle- and upper-income people moving back into the city, anything that detracted from the attractiveness of the city for those people was a mistake.

The City Council tried using a variety of decision-making techniques to sort out priorities and to give direction to the staff in making reductions. The longer this process went on, the more confusing it became and the more conflicts developed among Council members. The Council concluded that the services the city had been providing were all necessary, that they had been established to meet still existing needs, and that the only sensible way to apply cost reductions was across the board. The staff was directed to make such reductions and to be prepared to defend its rationale in making them.

The first step had already been taken to reduce the budget deficit. An employment freeze, imposed in the early summer, had already reduced payroll costs by eliminating positions that were then vacant. As a result, the number of layoffs that had to be made was substantially lower. In addition to not filling vacancies, 532 other employees were laid off, and an established goal of a total reduction of 1,000 employees at the end of two years was accomplished.

The layoffs included employees from all city general fund departments. The prohibition against filling vacant positions for any reason covered not only the general fund activities of the city but those that were financed in other ways. A manpower control committee, chaired initially by the budget director, was given the power to authorize the filling of a job vacancy, if a good enough case could be made for it. In practice, the red tape, delay, and aggravation involved in getting approval to fill a vacancy were so great that few but the most important vacancies were filled.

At the end of the budget year, all positions that were vacant were eliminated from the budget, if they had not been exempted from the freeze by the manpower control committee. This allowed the budget office to abolish supervisory positions, in contrast to the layoffs where only entry-level positions were eliminated. The manpower control committee became expert at dealing with departments that wanted to fill vacancies, and the department directors who served on the committee had a better understanding of budget restrictions and manpower needs throughout the city government.

The committee also served as a forum at which labor cost-reduction methods could be discussed and shared. The manpower control committee was so effective that after the first group of layoffs the manpower reduction goals were met without further layoffs, and the number of supervisory positions declined in proportion to the elimination of entry-level jobs.

One of the keys to the effectiveness of the manpower control committee was its makeup. At its beginning, the committee was established as a short-range expedient to deal with the problems created by the policy of eliminating vacant jobs. Its members were appointed by the City Manager with little regard for whether or not the individual department director wanted to serve. The Budget Director served as the committee's first chairman and established the procedures the committee followed.

When it became apparent that the committee would be a permanent one and that it served not only to regulate manpower levels but to establish other manpower policy, a practice of rotating its members was started. Department directors left the committee when they wanted to, and new members were selected on the basis of their willingness to volunteer. The manpower control committee's decisions were made after open debate often involving a number of department directors. This practice discouraged several department directors, whose applications to fill vacancies had been rejected, from appealing either to the City Manager or to the City Council. In most cases, the City Manager and City Council respected the decisions of the manpower control committee.

Community support for the administration's plan to reduce costs by an immediate reduction in the number of city employees by layoff, to be followed by a gradual further reduction of employment levels through attrition, was reflected in a cartoon in the morning newspaper. It showed the City Manager pushing a large individual labeled "city government" into a steam cabinet, with the help of "Mr. Cincinnati," who was saying to the city government, "relax, and enjoy it." Despite this and other demonstrations of approval, the City Manager and his staff knew that this support would cease if a general decline occurred in either the extent or quality of city services. In order to prevent such a decline in service levels or to minimize the effect of such a decline where it could not be prevented, the city began an examination of all its activities. As a result, a number of strategies were developed to deal with the problem of providing adequate city services despite a reduction in the city's workforce.

The options available to do this probably vary from city to city, but a list of examples of what Cincinnati was able to accomplish may serve as a framework for other city governments to evaluate the ability to reduce workforces without lowering the quality and extent of their services. The divisions of the following discussion are arbitrary, and the examples of the application of each category of change are only illustrative, not comprehensive. However, they suggest areas for study in any attempt to emulate Cincinnati's successful effort to reduce its municipal costs.

If the city doesn't do it, does someone else have to? Even though it had no legal requirement to perform some services, the city had for one reason or another taken them on, even though some other level of government was mandated to perform them. The best example of this was the city's weights and measurement checking operation. State statutes made this activity the responsibility of county government and provided for city regulation only if the city government wanted to do it. Cincinnati had assumed the responsibility of weights and measurement checking because it believed it could do a better job than the county government was doing. The fact was that the city did do a more thorough job than the county, but county residents seemed as satisfied with the service they received as did city residents. The city decided to discontinue its service and to encourage the county government to do a more thorough job in regulating weights and measurement. In effect, the city found the state legislature had given it the power to regionalize the cost of this service by ceasing to do it.

Can you get the state to shift the burden of providing a service to another level of government? Some of the services the state had mandated to the city in the past were now more equitably supplied with a governmental jurisdiction with a broader tax base. The clearest example of this was the Hamilton County Municipal Court system. This court with countywide jurisdiction was operated and funded by the city of Cincinnati. At the time the city assumed this responsibility, most of the population of the county lived in the city and the court generated enough income to pay for its operation. Even though the majority of the county's population no longer lived in the city and the city tax-payers were funding the deficit in the court's operation, the city still operated the court system. Once these facts were understood by the City Council, it led a lobbying effort in the state legislature to transfer responsibility from the court to the county government. This effort was successful, and the city was relieved of a major financial burden.

Is there anything you are doing you can stop doing? Like the pyramids, city services once started go on forever, even if they no longer serve any public purpose. This lack of public purpose is sometimes hard to detect, because those employees who provide the service have converted its original purpose to one of providing them with jobs. Interviews with the recipients of the service, as well as utilization studies, can be helpful in spotting those services that are candidates for elimination.

Cincinnati had provided a setout service as part of its refuse collection operation for some years. A crew of refuse collection employees preceded the collection crews through the district carrying homeowners' refuse to the curb. This service had been eliminated in an earlier budget cut, only to be restored after the voters approved a tax increase. Its elimination was one of the first cuts the Department of Public Works proposed and one of the first proposed reductions to produce a demonstration in the council chamber.

The demonstrators were community organizers who believed the elderly and the unwell could not carry out their refuse and that discontinuance of this service would create a real hardship for those groups. This point of view was reinforced by the unions who represented the employees who would be affected if the service were discontinued.

Fortunately, the budget officer had done some surveying that revealed only a minority of Cincinnati's citizens were using the service and that, in fact, a majority did not know it existed. The survey also found that a number of residents did not want city employees in their garages or backyards and had rejected the service. The City Council, when it realized that only a relatively small number of residents wanted or used the setout service, concurred in its elimination, with the provision that where there was a doctor's certificate stating that a resident was unable to carry out his trash, the city would perform this service.

The council also encouraged the administration to help a minority businessman institute a service that would set out refuse for a modest fee. It is interesting to note that very few citizens presented a health certificate and that the business founded to provide setout service soon went out of business for lack of customers. It was apparent that the setout service was not one very many citizens would have chosen if they had to pay for it.

Can you pay someone else less to provide a service than it costs you to do yourself? Although it may not be politically possible or always wise to contract out fire service or refuse collecting, there are a number of areas where contracting services to the private sector can reduce costs without creating other problems. An example was Cincinnati's contract to provide glass and muffler services to the municipal garage. The city had previously purchased mufflers and glass for city vehicles and installed them in the municipal garage. Because the city had not developed an effective cost-accounting system, no one realized how much this service cost. Once this cost figure was discovered, it did not take long to secure competitive bids from the private sector for replacing mufflers and broken glass. The costs the private bids revealed were so much lower than the city's costs that several contracts for providing annual service were entered into. Not only was it cheaper but the city found it was more convenient and that equipment was returned to service more promptly.

Can you get someone to volunteer to provide the service? The single most overlooked source of municipal cost reduction is the use of volunteers. Volunteers are often better qualified than regular employees and are many times more enthusiastic about the work they do. Volunteers also offer a vehicle for citizen involvement that is more productive than citizen activism, which often degenerates into single-issue lobbying.

As part of its recreation program, Cincinnati's recreation

department promoted golf tournaments at its municipal golf courses. The object of these tournaments was to increase the use of the municipal courses and to promote golf as a recreational activity for the citizens of the city. The tournaments, operated by the city's golf professionals, had been quite successful and popular. The recreation department decided to eliminate the professional direction of these tournaments and turn their operation over to a volunteer group of golfers. Not only did this reduce municipal costs but it improved the public acceptance of the tournaments.

Do charges for services reflect the true cost of providing that service? The charges made for a number of services, such as building inspection, recreation fees, and licensing, often reflect what other cities charge, not the real cost of the service. It may not always be possible to charge the full cost of providing a service, but at least you should know the real cost of the service.

In Cincinnati, the city provided inspection services for the installation and maintenance of elevators. The charge for this service covered less than one-half of the cost of providing it, and any attempt to raise the fee was bitterly resisted by the elevator repair and installation companies. Because it could not recover the cost of providing this service, the city decided to turn elevator inspection service over to the state. One of the arguments made whenever the city attempted to raise its fees for this service was that state fees were already lower than the city fees. When the city announced its intention of transferring elevator inspection to the state, the elevator installers and maintenance companies immediately petitioned the city to raise its fees and to continue the inspection service. The state workload was so great that inspections were often delayed, which increased the costs of the firms doing elevator work.

Are you recovering the full overhead costs for those programs that generate their own revenue? Because most city accounting systems are not designed to accurately reflect the true and total costs of providing a service, overhead costs are often overlooked or understated. Understatement of overhead cost is particularly prevalent in city revenue-producing activities. Cincinnati, after examining the total cost of providing services to its income-producing activities, began increasing overhead charges for them. The result was to increase the monies available to the general fund with, in most cases, modest increases in the charge for services.

Are you spending money to regulate some things that could best be deregulated? A number of city regulatory services were begun for the protection of a monopoly or a profession, and not for the benefit of the city's citizens. Despite the protestations of the regulatory staff that it is for the public good, the result of regulation is often to limit the supply of a service and to drive its price up. The regulation of the number of taxicabs in Cincinnati is an example of this control of supply. A partially successful attempt was made to end the regulation of the number of taxicabs and to eliminate the regulatory staff. The number of licenses was increased, but the regulation remained, and the city continued to spend money for this unnecessary service.

Can you invest capital to reduce operating costs? Because most city budgets are developed on a yearly basis, little attempt is made to use capital expenditures to reduce long-term operating costs. It is often easier to secure funding for a $15,000-a-year job that may go on forever than to buy a machine that costs $25,000 but will eliminate the need for an employee. Cincinnati prepared a five-year budget and developed a procedure for analyzing the relationship of capital expenditures to operating costs.

An example of the savings made possible by this approach was the replacement of the city's refuse collection fleet. The average age of the city's current fleet was more than seven years, and the equipment had been designed to operate on hard surfaces when the city was using incinerators. The age of the equipment, coupled with the breakdowns that occurred when the vehicles were operating at the landfill, meant that equipment was constantly out of service and it was necessary for the city to pay overtime to get the refuse collected. Rather than postpone buying new equipment, the city purchased a fleet of heavy-duty trucks with high-compaction bodies that were designed for the conditions under which the equipment would be operating. The result was to reduce the overtime costs, the repair costs, and the frustration of customers about late service.

Can you reduce costs and maintain or increase productivity by establishing work standards? Most of the standards that have been developed for municipal services are not very useful in attempting to reduce municipal costs and will, if applied, probably increase costs rather than reduce them. Knowing the number of books your library needs per hundred thousand of population, or the amount of parkland that fits the standard set by the park professionals, or the number of fire fighters required under the old grading schedule won't help a bit in reducing costs, and will probably only provide ammunition for those who oppose cuts in their favorite municipal services.

What is needed is a set of work-related standards that measures the present work output of a workforce and identifies ways to increase work output. Development of such a set of standards will reveal problems that reduce productivity and will help employees set goals for improving their performance. Cincinnati's experience in developing work standards revealed that poor management was responsible for more poor work performance than was employees' unwillingness to work harder.

The city's highway maintenance division, which was responsible for the maintenance of road and bridge structures, as well as street sweeping and snow removal, used its labor-management committee as the means to develop work standards in that division. The superintendent of the highway maintenance division and the president of the union that represented the employees of that division agreed to a program to develop work standards that involved both the workers in the division and management. The first step in this program was to ask employees about their jobs to identify what impediments they thought reduced their productivity. Unreliable equipment, poor scheduling, and inadequate training were identified as problems. All could be solved by management without changing work rules or without major expenditures of city money.

Management in the highway maintenance division began to implement changes designed to correct the problems that were identifed by the employees. When these changes began, the employees realized that their ideas were being taken seriously, and they cooperated in developing work standards designed to measure the improvements that resulted from changes made by management. The standards developed seemed reasonable to most of the personnel of the division. They were perceived to have come from the ideas of the workers and not to have been imposed by a higher level of management. What had been a contest of trying to fix the blame for poor performance became a cooperative effort to increase the quality and quantity of the work of the division. Despite a substantial manpower reduction in the highway maintenance division, the amount of work performed by the division increased by a measurable 10 percent by the end of the first year of the application of this work standards program.

Is there or can one build a mechanical device that will reduce labor costs? During the last 15 years, the federal government has spawned a number of programs to transfer the "technology that put a man on the moon" to solving the problems of city government. Consultants, organizations representing city governments, or the people employed by them, and research groups have used the money provided by the federal government to set up consortiums, user groups, corporations, and institutes to identify municipal problems that are susceptible to the application of technology and to develop solutions to them, using technology developed as a part of various federal programs. Even though the product of all this effort doesn't live up to the promises made at its start, there have been a number of useful products developed, ranging from an automatic fire pumper control to a one-man garbage truck.

It is worthwhile to city operations to see if there may be an application for a number of these devices. A city may also find it can develop its own technological solution to an operating problem. Cincinnati developed its own solution to the problem of reducing the cost of emptying street waste containers. The city had been using a standard rear-end loader with a crew of three to empty the trash containers located in the downtown area. By changing the design of the containers, the city found it could use a modified catch-basin cleaner to empty them. A one-man crew replaced the three-man crew, and, because that man did not need to get out of his truck to empty the containers, he was safer in downtown traffic and could work faster.

Is your capital program designed to reduce operating and maintenance costs, or will it increase them? Because most municipal capital programs are geared to a longer period of time than is the operating budget, projects may be in the pipeline that upon completion will compound the problem of trying to reduce the operating budget. Often capital programs reflect planning strategies that were developed to cope with problems such as growth that no longer exist. Careful examination of the city's capital program may reveal opportunities to stop projects that will raise operating costs and to redirect monies to cost-reduction activities. It may be embarrassing to admit you paid for land or plans you are not going to use, but it is a lot better than completing a project only to find that you can't afford to operate it. Cincinnati was able to turn around a fire station replacement project by a better siting program that allowed it to abandon two old fire stations for every new one it opened. A number of fire companies were eliminated without much sacrifice in fire coverage or service.

Do you own any property that you could return to the tax rolls by either selling it or giving it away? Most cities own a number of pieces of property that are left over from street widening projects, tax foreclosures, or abandoned projects that are a problem to keep clean and safe. These could be sold or given away and returned to private ownership and the tax rolls. Cincinnati developed a computer listing of all its property (some of which it did not know it owned) by consulting the county's property ownership records. These properties were classified into three groups: those that the city wanted to keep for one reason or another; those that had a commercial value; and those that had so little value they were best given to the adjoining property owners. An aggressive program was started for selling salable properties and giving away those that were not salable. It resulted in a number of properties being returned to the tax rolls, generating additional city income. A bonus was a reduction in the city's cost of maintaining its properties.

This list of cost-reduction techniques used by the city of Cincinnati may help to develop cost-reducing programs in other cities, by using the same ideas or by developing new ones.

7

IMPROVING PRODUCTIVITY

THE DECEMBER 1978 General Accounting Office (GAO) report to the Congress on state and local government productivity improvement defines productivity as "the relationship between resources used and results achieved." Improvement in productivity means "either (1) obtaining more and better program output from a given level of resources, or (2) using fewer resources to maintain or improve a certain quality level of program output."[1]

That report concludes that state and local government productivity is not nearly as high as it could be, especially when compared with private sector organizations. This low productivity has led, in many cases, to higher costs of government and/or lower levels of service.

The principal reason for low state and local government productivity is the lack of a "profit motive." Other factors include the labor intensiveness of local government services; political and special interest group pressures, including unions; lack of public interest in "nebulous" goals such as productivity improvement; civil service protections; and lack of ways to adequately measure government outputs.

Productivity doesn't merely mean finding ways to make

[1] U.S. General Accounting Office, *State and Local Government Productivity Improvement: What Is the Federal Role?* Report to the Congress of the United States. Washington, D.C.: U.S. GAO, December 6, 1978.

local government employees work harder or faster. It includes activities such as:

- Arranging work so that wasteful motion and effort are eliminated;
- Making sense of the maze of forms, procedures, and overlapping activities which too often characterizes government;
- Analyzing, streamlining, and simplifying the business of government; and
- Discarding processes or programs made obsolete by new technologies and/or changing needs.[2]

Productivity can be improved by strengthening management, by functional or structural reorganization, by introducing new technology, and/or by increasing worker motivation. The GAO report concluded that "most state and local governments need some kind of externally provided technical assistance and information to sustain and support productivity efforts partly because of the lack of in-house technical staff."[3]

Strategies for improving productivity can be developed as a result of outside stimuli, as the GAO report suggests, but they can also be initiated internally by city councils, city managers, or department heads. Categories of productivity improvement include the following:

1. Reorganizing services.
2. Increasing employee motivation.
3. Employing new technologies.
4. Improving work standards, measurement, and scheduling.

Productivity improvements can be made in every functional area of local government activities as well as in general management and planning. This chapter will examine the strategy of service reorganization in depth by reviewing general police-

---

[2] George P. Barbour, Jr., "Improving Productivity for Better Service Delivery: A View from the Council Chamber." *Management Information Service Report.* Washington, D.C.: International City Management Association, June 1976, p. 2.

[3] U.S. GAO, *op. cit.,* p. 30.

fire consolidation efforts. In addition, it discusses examples of using differing productivity improvement techniques.

REORGANIZING SERVICES

The strategy of reorganizing services involves consolidation or rearrangement of services so that existing resources are used more effectively. For example, in Fairfax County, Virginia, a study of building inspectors' activities resulted in the establishment of nine field offices throughout the county. Inspectors, who once reported daily to the central County Administration Building, now report to the office closest to their inspection and, to the extent possible, to their homes. This has resulted in significant savings in fuel consumption and has increased the amount of time available for inspections by about 20 percent.

A much more radical service reorganization strategy is the consolidation of police and fire services into a general public safety operation. Such major consolidations are not easy to effect, but they can offer significant benefits under certain conditions. A detailed discussion of several police-fire consolidations follows.

POLICE-FIRE CONSOLIDATION[4]

City fire and police departments are steeped in many years of traditional service. Such tradition can be the source of strong resistance to any proposed changes in the frame of reference in which these services operate. Generally, traditional fire and police operations have been appraised as adequate. Why, then, would a city administrator wish to change or consolidate these two departments? Mounting public pressures for better protection, combined with limited funds, have forced city officials to consider nontraditional organizational designs for these services, because they may be less costly and equally or more effective.

---

[4] John J. Berry, "Fire-Police Consolidation," unpublished paper. Raleigh: North Carolina State University, May 5, 1973.

Cities throughout the United States have continued to experience accelerated population growth, demographic shifts from rural to urban areas, and rapidly changing housing and industrial development patterns. Today, crime and fire represent major social problems in urban areas. Most statistics project an increase in these problems for the future. Public pressure has mounted for better protective services. While traditional methods have been less than totally effective, the major concern today is how to meet increasing needs for protection with the limited resources available.

The salaries of public employees constitute about 85 percent of the average city's budget. It is expected that this rate of growth will increase substantially in the years ahead. There has been an upward adjustment in salaries and fringe benefits in the private sector. The 72-hour duty week for fire department personnel has been reduced to a 56-hour week, and it is expected that they will soon demand a 42-hour week.

One area that has always frustrated the city administrator is how to utilize firemen during their nonproductive time. A study in San Diego, California, showed that 67 percent of each fireman's duty time was unproductive, that only 1.3 percent was used in responding to fires, and that 9.2 percent was used for routine maintenance or reconditioning equipment. Similar studies in Evanston, Illinois; Glencoe, Illinois; Greensboro, North Carolina; and Los Angeles, California, produced results paralleling the San Diego study.[5] The tremendous importance of the fire fighter during short periods has made such situations acceptable until today when revenues are shrinking.

Rising expenditures, budgetary limitations, and a demand by the public for better services have forced the city administrator to seek new methods to provide effective and efficient protective services. Some form of fire-police consolidation may be a viable alternative.

A city needs to plan carefully and follow sound implementation procedures to attain the goals of a better protective

[5] Harry W. More, Jr., *The New Era of Public Safety.* Springfield, Ill.: Charles C Thomas, 1970, p. 50.

service through consolidation. The differing needs of various communities must be satisfied to complete a successful reorganization. Many factors must be considered before a course of action can be selected. Among these are demographic, political, economic, and social characteristics of the community, with an interest toward the forecasted changes they will experience.

Changing land-use patterns of the community and surrounding area have great significance in determining public safety requirements. Physical boundaries of rivers, lakes, and mountains affect growth patterns as do man-made facilities such as freeways, bridges, and railways. The location, type, and age of residential, industrial, and commercial buildings also help determine the type and amount of protection needed.

Community economic characteristics will also help determine the resources that may be available to an administrator considering the organizational change. The decision to unify services should not be made on cost and economy bases, but on effectiveness and efficiency outputs. However, the communities' ability and willingness to pay provide the administrator a sphere of operation and establish his limitations.

Total population by age, sex, birth and death rates, race, population density, migration, and tourist habits all have an influence on public safety requirements. They should be evaluated carefully when making reorganization plans. Statistical analysis should be made of past fire and police incidents. Trends in types and locations of fires, rescue calls, false alarms, criminal offenses, motor vehicle accidents, and arrests are beneficial to the planner to aid in anticipation of future needs.

All communities will not have every alternative available to them. State constitutions, pension regulations, statutes regulating pay, statutory definitions of police and fire personnel, statutes regulating working conditions, city charters, municipal ordinances, and civil service regulations may in some way restrict a desired objective and necessitate changes in regulations or statutes. A thorough review should be made of all legal documents to determine what can and cannot be done.

Not all forces accept consolidation as the best alternative

to better protection. Therefore, opposition from certain pressure groups can be expected to any proposal for unification.
Police opposition is generally local in nature. The International
Association of Chiefs of Police has never taken an official position on the issue. On the other hand, the International Association of Fire Fighters has been strongly opposed to consolidation. This opposition stems from union-related activities. If
intense opposition persists at the local level from the police
and/or fire fighters, the success of consolidation is doubtful at
best.

Types of consolidation

Efforts to consolidate police and fire services under various
titles and in varying degrees have a long history, dating from
27 B.C. when the first Emperor of Rome, Augustus, created the
virgiles. This large group of men, armed with batons and short
swords, was responsible for keeping the peace and fighting
fires.[6] The degree to which public safety services are consolidated in the United States can be classified in five distinct categories: consolidated services, partial consolidation, selected
area consolidation, functional consolidation, and nominal consolidation. The only importance in establishing categories is to
be able to study the elements that make up each system. A category should not be used by a city as a model for reorganization. Each city has its own peculiarities and a system should be
tailored to fit these differences.

Consolidated services. The identifying feature of the consolidated services organization is a single administrator responsible
for both fire and police services. The key factor is the single
staff for the unified service. The line function is usually divided
into three departments—fire, patrol, and detective. The majority of the members of the force receive cross-training in both
fire-fighting and police duties. A major segment of this force
performs generalist duties where emphasis can be placed on in-

[6] *Ibid.,* p. 28.

tensified patrol and preventive activities. Walter L. Webb of the International City Management Association says, "This degree of consolidation is best suited to smaller communities and will, in all probability, be implemented most easily in rapidly expanding or newly created communities."[7]

Partial consolidation. The features of partial consolidation are that each fire and police service retains its own identity. A special patrol unit is formed that performs both police and fire duties. A dual line of command extends from the fire and police departments; when the patrol is engaged in fire fighting, it receives instructions from the fire chief; when engaged in police duties, the police chief directs the patrol unit. "This type of consolidation can accommodate both the customary separation of the protective services and assignment of selected personnel to positions where they can be more effectively used."[8]

Selected area consolidation. The selected area consolidation method is similar to partial consolidation in that the same features are present (that is, separate services and special patrols used to conduct fire and police duties). The difference is that these patrols are limited in operation to selected geographic areas of the city. The advantages of this method are that it can be expanded as the city acquires new territories and there are no limits to the size of the community that can use it.

Functional consolidation. Functional consolidation uses a different approach than the first three cited. The previous methods used the patrol unit to consolidate the fire-police duties. The individual was identified as a public safety officer. In functional consolidation, each fire-police service retains its own identity, but one or more duties assigned to one department is assumed by the other. The fire fighters, having the most "free time," are usually assigned additional duties in the police department. This would appear to create a morale problem for the fire department; however, it has been used successfully

---

[7] Walter L. Webb, "Unified Public Safety Operations." *Management Information Service Report.* Washington, D.C.: International City Management Association, March 1972, p. 2.
[8] *Ibid.*

throughout the United States. It has no restriction as to the size of a city but is especially adaptable to smaller communities. *Nominal consolidation.* The nominal consolidation method is used to group the functions of safety into one agency. The merger of these functions occurs at the top of the organization in the form of a Public Safety Director. Consolidation does not extend down through the organization, as each department continues to operate as a separate unit. This method has not made an impact on the fire-police problem. It could be considered useful as preparation for adopting one of the other methods.

After weighing all factors mentioned here, if it has been decided that a particular degree of consolidation is suitable for a community, a plan for installation must be devised. The plan for implementation should address legal, leadership, personnel, training, and equipment aspects. The next section discusses the experiences of three cities that selected unification.

Case study: Winston-Salem, North Carolina[9]

The rapid population growth of Winston-Salem has kept pace with other urban areas in North Carolina. The 1950 census placed the city's population at 88,000. In 1957, the population was estimated to be 108,000, and in 1968 it had grown to 132,-000. Natural increase, in-migration, and major annexations to the city accounted for these gains. In 1968, the city covered 57.4 square miles. The community's economic base is consumer goods industries made up of the manufacture of tobacco products, hosiery and other wearing apparel, telephone equipment, and furniture. Banking is a major industry and a large university community is present.

After an annexation in 1957, a new fire company (No. 8) was activated. Then, in 1964, with further annexation, company No. 9 became necessary. With this rapid growth and its forecasted continued growth, it was readily apparent that ad-

---

[9] Allen Joines, *The History of Fire-Police Cooperation in the City of Winston-Salem, N.C., 1957–1972.* Unpublished report, March 1972.

ditional requirements for public safety protection would be needed. The City Manager believed the city was outstripping its ability to pay for adequate fire and police protection in conventional ways. In February 1957, he submitted a proposal to the Board of Aldermen and received approval to activate fire company No. 8 on an experimental basis to test the concept of the fire-police patrol. The test was to be for six months and was confined to a selected residential area.

Fourteen men were assigned to Company No. 8; four of these men were on duty at any one time; two were at the fire station ready to drive the pumper truck, and the other two were on patrol duty. Six regular fire fighters were assigned to fire station duty and worked the same hours as the fire department. The other eight men who were assigned to patrol duty received training both as fire fighters and law enforcement officers and worked police department hours. Members of the fire-police patrol were recognized first as fire fighters and second as police officers. They were under the supervision of the fire company officer on duty.

An evaluation regarding the operation of the fire-police function was made for the period from September 9, 1957 to March 21, 1958. The City Manager recommended to the Board of Aldermen that the fire-police patrol be continued on a permanent basis, and, as new fire companies were activated, that the fire-police patrol be strongly considered. At this time, the board give the fire-police patrol a permanent status in the city's public safety program. When Station No. 9 became necessary in 1964, it was activated as a fire-police patrol unit.

The original fire-police cooperative program proved its effectiveness in both fire fighting and police work at a substantial saving to the taxpayers. In July 1965, it was estimated that the operation of the two fire-police units produced an annual saving in excess of $70,000.

Winston-Salem's pilot program had given impetus to the consideration of a total public safety officers' program for the city. If effectiveness could be increased and costs of operation could be lowered on a small scale, it might be possible to accomplish increased benefits on a larger scale. Experience in other cities that had public safety programs seemed to substantiate this. In December 1971, the Assistant City Manager for Operations presented a draft plan of a public safety officers' program to the Board of Aldermen, the Fire Department, the Police Department, and City Management staff members.

Opposition to the plan came from the Winston-Salem Fire Fighters, Inc. Major criticisms presented were (1) consolidation would break up the company unit, thus hampering the coordination and ultimately the efficiency of the unit; (2) results of previous consolidation attempts had caused poor morale and lowered fire-fighting efficiency; (3) the plan was seen as an expansion of police coverage at the expense of eliminating on-duty fire companies; (4) administrative problems would result in a struggle between the two departments; and (5) the plan was seen as lowering fire protection while improving police service. The majority of criticisms were believed to result from a lack of understanding about the plan. The Assistant City Manager scheduled meetings and talks with the fire fighters, and many of their ideas and suggestions were incorporated into the final plan. The Winston-Salem Firemen's Association finally voted by a narrow margin to support the public safety program.

The Board of Aldermen approved a public safety program for Winston-Salem on February 7, 1972. This new plan was developed on the basis of reducing the strength of the conventional fire station but backing it up with a public safety division. The city was divided into three districts with three fire stations in each district, as shown in Figure 7. A public safety supervisor and three public safety officers are assigned to each district. The supervisor answers to the watch commander in the police department and the assistant chief on duty in the fire department.

The public safety division is the basic unit in the organization. It has police and fire responsibilities within a geographic area. The division consists of 48 men, 12 public safety supervisors, and 36 public safety officers. The 48 men stand eight-hour

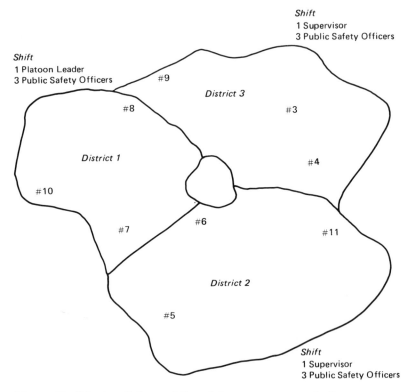

Figure 7. Winston-Salem public safety program organization.

shifts for an average workweek of 42 hours. The on-duty team consists of 12 men, one supervisor, and three officers in each district.

The public safety officer is a fireman-policeman who is trained, equipped, and prepared to respond immediately to any fire or police incident. Work performed during an eight-hour shift falls into three categories: emergency work, fire and police patrol, and preschedule nonemergency.

A public safety supervisor is in command of the 12-man on-duty team. His most important function is to coordinate all operations in all three districts in fire fighting and police work. He also supervises personnel in nonemergency work such as prefire inspection, training, and care of vehicles. During their eight-hour shift, personnel are responsible for special assignments, patrol vehicles, and records.

Administratively, the division is under the dual direction of both the fire department and the police department, depending on the type of work the safety officer is performing. The Assistant Fire Chief directs activities during emergency fire duty, and the Police Watch Commander is in charge for police duties.

Substantial benefits from this arrangement are that it

1. *Improves fire protection.* Public safety officers are usually at the scene of a fire before the fire equipment and sometimes have the fire under control before the equipment arrives. In some cases, the fire was discovered during a patrol.
2. *Improves police protection.* The additional 12 patrol cars increase the police patrol strength by 45 to 60 percent. This new force assumes 24.8 percent of the police department's work of patrolling and answering calls and covers 60 to 80 percent of the city's land area.
3. *Facilitates prevention programs.* Fire inspection programs can be enlarged. A greater show of force has a strong effect on deterring criminal activities. Public education concerning public safety can be conducted.
4. *Confines cost of operations.* Providing this additional protection has cost the city $84,000 annually. To achieve the same benefits under the traditional fire and police organizations would require an annual budget increase of $275,000 (1973 figures).

Case study: Durham, North Carolina[10]

The City of Durham has experienced growth and expansion similar to Winston-Salem's. In the 1960 census, its population totaled 78,302. In 1970, the population had increased to 95,438.

---

[10] Esai Berenbaum, Director of Public Safety, Durham, N.C., private interview, February 12, 1973.

The city is noted for many cigarette factories and cotton-textile and hosiery mills. It is also the home of Duke University.

In 1968, the City Manager proposed to the City Council the merger of two fire companies and two patrol units with fire-police responsibilities for a selected geographic area. The proposal met with strong opposition, spearheaded by the International Association of Fire Chiefs. The general manager of this association, in a speech to the City Council, contended the plan would create chaos rather than give fire protection. Opposition was so strong that the plan was dropped.

In 1970, the city faced two serious problems that required action. The first problem was associated with the reduction of the average workweek of the fire fighters from 72 to 56 hours. This problem was not unique to Durham as other North Carolina cities had been required to reduce their workweek to 52 hours. In the northeastern United States, 42-hour workweeks are common. This reduction in hours would have required 47 additional fire fighters for the city at a cost of $400,000 with no improvement in fire protection.

The second problem was mounting public pressure for additional police protection. Among the ten largest cities of North Carolina, Durham ranked ninth in number of police employees in proportion to population. Durham's crime index was the fourth worst in North Carolina.

The public safety program for Durham was inaugurated in January 1971. The organization that followed took the form of a consolidated service. A Public Safety Director was appointed, with the fire chief and the police chief reporting directly to him. Fire-Police Departments retained certain conventional elements, but five of the seven fire stations were authorized to become public safety stations. Control of the public safety companies was a dual function of the Fire-Police Departments. The duty being performed determined the source of supervision. Administratively, the public safety officers were placed under the Police Department.

In the fiscal year 1970–1971 budget, 220 personnel were authorized in the Police Department and 158 in the Fire Department, for a total of 378 personnel. The fiscal year

1972–1973 budget authorized 227 personnel in the Police Department and 122 in the Fire Department for a total of 349. Of the 150 in the police patrol division, 120 are public safety officers, all of whom have received 16 weeks of combined police-fire training.

Four of the seven fire stations are now operating as public safety stations. The other three are in the "high-risk," central business district and continue to operate as conventional fire stations. There are no plans to convert the remaining three fire stations to public safety stations. There is, however, a new public safety station planned for a growing residential/commercial area.

Each public safety station is manned by a five-man crew of fire-police trained personnel. Each crew consists of a supervisor, two patrolmen, and two men in the station who operate the fire truck and maintain equipment. The supervisor and two of his men patrol in three cars a designated area adjacent to the station that performs police duties. A minimum of three men is required at a serious fire. Thus, two of the patrol cars could be occupied and the team could still meet the minimum requirements at the fire scene. Actual practice has found the average response to fire calls is higher than four men per call.

Before the inauguration of the present program, it required 80 personnel (fire and police) to man the four fire stations and provide five patrol cars. The public safety operation now covers these same areas with 11 patrol cars and, including the manning of the stations, utilizes only 76 men.

Through December 1972, the public safety companies had answered 867 fire calls without significant conflict with their law enforcement duties. Only 4 percent of these calls were serious fires, 24 percent required a fire truck present (the fire truck responded many times when not required), and one or two public safety officers handled 76 percent of all calls.

The public safety program was not envisioned as a money-saving operation but, rather, to provide improved police and fire protection within the confines of monetary constraints.

Many benefits were realized by the city:

1. Police patrol is strengthened by an average of about eight men per shift (36 percent increase).
2. In the high-crime period between 6 P.M. and 11 P.M., police patrol is strengthened by 13 men (60 percent increase).
3. The number of off-duty patrolmen (public safety officers) subject to call for major law enforcement situations is increased by 42 men.
4. Fire-fighting on-duty strength is increased from 48 to 50 men.
5. The number of off-duty fire fighters (and public safety officers) subject to call for major fires is doubled (163 as compared to 81).
6. Duty hours for fire fighters are reduced from 72 to 56 per week, and for public safety officers pulling fire duty work, only 42 hours per week.

Case Study; Peoria, Illinois[11]

The implementation of fire-police consolidation in two cities discussed previously appears to have been successful. The following is a study of a city that has had eight years' experience in a partial consolidation and has returned to conventional fire-police services.

Peoria is an industrial and urban municipality in central Illinois that in the 1970 census had a population of 126,000. In 1957, the Illinois Legislature passed a law limiting the working hours of all municipal fire fighters. The city sought relief from this additional financial burden by implementing a partial consolidation fire-police service in 1962. The program utilized police patrolmen as on-call fire fighters. The concept was that highly trained personnel from the police department would respond to fire calls to complement fire department personnel. It was thought that a cooperative police patrolman would be equivalent to a fully trained, full-time hoseman.

The major objective of the program was to save the city

---

[11] Gordon K. Zenk, "Police-Fire Consolidation." *Nation's Cities*, June 1972.

$225,000 a year by eliminating 40 men from the fire department. The program was authorized by the City Council in February 1962, overriding the strong objections of the Fire Chief and fire department members. Shortly thereafter, 39 fire fighters lost their jobs. Although the city realized a direct annual saving of $225,000 by eliminating these fire fighters, the citizens of Peoria experienced an estimated $4.4 million (for the eight-year period) in fire losses because of the inefficiency of the program. After a study and a recommendation by a private consulting firm to return to a conventional fire-police system, the city discontinued the consolidated system.

The failure of the system to provide the required services can be attributed to several reasons. The cooperative patrol was intended to be a highly trained group of personnel receiving higher pay because of more training and increased responsibility. In practice, the program did not operate in this manner. The system was a means to increase the pay for the police patrolman but he received very little additional training. Another shortcoming was that police districts did not coincide with fire districts, so there was confusion in responding to fires. This, coupled with the lack of a regular pattern of assigning patrolmen to designated districts forestalled the development of teamwork necessary for fire fighting. These factors contributed to the low morale of the fire fighters. They spent much of their time gathering statistics to verify the inefficiency of the system.

It is easy to see why the program did not give Peoria the desired benefits. It was inaugurated primarily to save money rather than as a means to improve protection for the community. This saving was at the expense of the fire department, which in turn strongly resisted the program. The failure of the police department to ensure proper training for its personnel or adjust conventional methods to the new concept doomed the program to failure.

Comparisons. Winston-Salem and Durham experienced constant population growth and land expansion from 1950 to 1970. During the same period, Peoria decreased in population from 111,856 in 1950 to 103,162 in 1960 and its program was launched in 1962. Peoria's population increased to 126,963 in 1970. It is probable that consolidation is more palatable and acceptable in a growing and expanding residential community.

All of the three cities faced opposition from various fire associations. Peoria is located in an area where trade unions are legal and more united in their efforts. This opposition was never overcome because subsequent events supported union criticisms. Winston-Salem and Durham had the same opposition but lacked the strong union resistance because North Carolina statutes prohibit local government unions. They were able to work with the local units, and issues that could not be resolved were at least neutralized.

It appears that the leadership in the two North Carolina cities was more effective than in the Illinois city. Plans for implementation, operational procedures, and training programs were of major concern to the ranking city official. The support of these top officials made the program work.

Training programs in Peoria seemed to be nonexistent, whereas in Winston-Salem and Durham all personnel received initial training and were evaluated before assuming duty as a public safety officer. It was during this period that positive attitudes toward the program were developed. Aggressive in-service training programs have continued.

There are some differences in the Winston-Salem and Durham programs. Winston-Salem has chosen partial and selected area consolidation, and Durham has chosen consolidated services. The main difference has been in the organizations. The functions of the individual public safety officer at the working level are similar. That one city selected one method and the other city selected another can be attributed mostly to city official preference. Both are working successfully in their own location.

Summary. The consolidation of fire and police services is not a panacea for a community. It is, however, an alternative that should be considered by city officials who face increasing protection needs and limited or shrinking resources. Several significant factors contribute to its effectiveness. The size of the city is one of these factors. The larger the fire-police departments, the stronger the emphasis is on separatism and functional specialization. This is reenforced by many employees affiliated with unions. It is evident, however, that some form of consolidation is adaptable to a city of any size. Communities that are small in size and growing fast, and/or communities that have large residential areas can readily use consolidated services. These communities have in common a limited source of revenue and large areas of protective service responsibility. Unification of fire-police forces may be a particularly compelling alternative in communities experiencing high crime rates and where more policemen are needed but budgets won't allow the additions. Such an approach must be supported by positive leadership, sufficient personnel, a good training program, modern operating procedures, and ample equipment.

OTHER PRODUCTIVITY IMPROVEMENT STRATEGIES

In addition to service reorganization, some other categories of productivity improvement will be briefly mentioned. These are (1) increasing employee motivation, (2) employing new technologies, and (3) setting work standards, establishing measures, and scheduling.

Employee motivation

Asking employees to suggest ways to improve productivity develops their participation and interest in the successful implementation of productivity improvement programs. The city of Rockville, Maryland, for example, created a productivity improvement task force of employees from its public works and recreation departments. The task force recommended a four-day, ten-hour workweek to increase the efficiency in vehicle servicing and to give employees longer weekends. As a result, more than $3,000 was saved in overtime costs.[12] This consulta-

[12] Connie Wright, "City Keeps Alive Productivity Unit As Federal Funds End." *Nation's Cities Weekly,* February, 19, 1979.

tive program, originally established by federal funds, was considered so useful that it was continued by the city even after the federal funds were exhausted.

Inglewood, California, instituted a flextime program for its city employees. Employees could choose when they would arrive between 7 and 9 A.M. and would leave eight hours later. This enabled the City Hall to be open to the public from 7:30 A.M. to 6 P.M. instead of from 8 to 5, without hiring new employees or paying estimated annual overtime costs of $20,000.[13]

Other well-known strategies related to employee motivation include organization development and team building, management by objectives, and the development of financial reward systems for employee-initiated productivity improvements.

New technologies

The identification and use of new technologies by local governments, as strategies for the 1980s, are treated at length in Chapter 8 of this book. It will be noted here that new technologies and the institution of new technical improvements are often effective means to improve productivity. Word processing systems and automated data processing are two well-known productivity improving options available to local governments.

New products, such as better street-cleaning or mowing machines or longer-lasting pothole patching materials, can be purchased to improve effectiveness and/or save service delivery dollars. To ensure fuel conservation, some cities have installed computer-based fuel dispensing systems in which users are issued credit cards, and transaction records for individual fuel consumption are maintained in a computer.

Refuse collection, street maintenance, and police and fire fighting are all areas in which new equipment advances become available daily. It is necesary first to find the most reli-

---

[13] Barbour, *op. cit.,* p. 3.

able and up-to-date source of information on such new products and processes. Then, one must develop the technical and political expertise to select those products or processes that are suited to a particular community's service delivery needs, while at the same time being politically palatable to groups such as unionized employees and citizens. Assistance in both of these tasks can be obtained from professional associations, such as the American Public Works Association, or assistance groups, such as regional innovation groups or state departments of community affairs. A city can hire or designate an in-house technology agent to review and evaluate productivity-enhancing products and processes and to make recommendations on the basis of costs, likely barriers to implementation, life of service, and personnel reductions possible.

Technological innovations have much to offer in the realm of productivity improvement. Their identification and implementation, however, can be complex and intricate from political or personnel standpoints. Thus, the productivity-improvement-minded manager of the 1980s is advised to be prepared to conduct sufficient prior review and to manage such efforts carefully so that benefits can be achieved without unforeseen, usually avoidable, complications.

Work standards, measurement, and scheduling

Many work measurement standards of both effectiveness and efficiency have been developed. Standards can be detailed time and motion studies, or they can be derived from more qualitative criteria, such as citizen perceptions or the visual appearance of streets and parks. For example, Fort Worth, Texas, instituted a program in which street sweeper supervisors act as trained observers to rate operator performance. The supervisors inform operators by radio of unsatisfactory performance and request resweeping. Supervisors' records become important components of employee performance records.

Many cities have developed computerized management information systems that inventory all streets and their characteristics (type, age, signs, surface conditions, usage, last maintenance). Such systems allow more efficient scheduling of street maintenance crews. Dallas, Texas, had a program in which time-lapse photography was used to improve the work methods of street patching and hydrant maintenance crews.

The city of Pasadena, California, has been a leader in developing productivity improvement strategies over the past five years. Pasadena's Productivity Management System (PMS) has these key elements: a management-by-objectives style of management; the creation of a management analysis function to identify areas that show promise for cost avoidance or improved productivity; and the development of files to be used for operations improvement.

The sequence of steps Pasadena has used for its Productivity Management System is as follows.

1. Establishment of work performance objectives.
2. Development of formal statements of planned approaches to accomplish objectives.
3. Measurement of performance.
4. Analyses of approaches and resulting outcomes.
5. Recommendations for change or improvement.
6. Implementation of change plans.

To carry out its program, Pasadena selected its Finance Department as the test bed for experimenting with productivity improvement. Training workshops dealing with setting objectives, auditing performance, and monitoring the behavioral side of operations improvement were scheduled for all management personnel. As a result, all departments prepared lists of measurable objectives for their activities.

In Phoenix, Arizona, the city initiated a comprehensive productivity improvement program in all city agencies. It included program evaluation, methods improvements, and work measurement. The costs of this program averaged $225,000 per year, but the resulting benefits were approximately $2.5 million per year.[14]

[14] *Ibid.,* p. 5.

CONCLUSION

The 1978 GAO report suggested several strategies to assist local governments with productivity improvement. It suggested that the Office of Personnel Management become the federal-level focal point for such assistance. It called for changes in the federal grant-in-aid system to remove barriers to local productivity and to build incentives as much as possible. These include reducing federal reporting and paperwork requirements; simplifying and standardizing federal "cross-cutting" requirements, such as environmental impact review, nondiscrimination, and planning; consolidating more categorical programs into block grants; and eliminating detailed requirements and controls if accountability for program results is established on quantitative measures.

If provisions of the Federal Grant and Cooperative Agreement Act (PL 95–224) were implemented, a review of all federal assistance programs could be undertaken to determine when the building in of performance incentives is necessary and when it is not. The GAO report considers that performance incentives are appropriate in programs where the federal government is having local and state governments carry out national objectives, such as water pollution control, but may be inappropriate for programs designed to provide financial help so that local and state governments can meet their own locally defined priorities, for example, reducing crime.

Federal efforts to remove the productivity disincentives from the grant-in-aid system are badly needed. In the end, however, local managers and local government personnel will provide the real impetus for productivity improvements that will pay off. Walter Balk has called for managers and employees in government to develop a "solid productivity ethic." This consists in spearheading the technical improvement of agency activities; improving decision-making capabilities; encouraging more employee participation; and influencing politicians and constituencies to make agency change "more possible, benign, and permanent." He states bluntly:

Public administrators have a fundamental choice. They will either lead the way or be dragged into the new, uneasy era of government parsimony and creative conservation.[15]

The 1980s is the decade for local officials and citizens to choose to adopt and promote such a productivity ethic.

[15] Walter L. Balk, "Toward A Government Productivity Ethic." *Public Administration Review*, January/February 1978, p. 50.

8

USING NEW TECHNOLOGIES

As has been discussed in previous chapters, there is little question that as local governments enter the decade of the 1980s they face one of the most critical periods in their entire existence. Numerous challenges are being made to the roles of local governments; to the type, level, and quality of the public services they provide; and to the efficiency with which these services are delivered. Local government administrations have never been under greater pressures from different sources and groups. Some administrators will leave the public administration field because of it; others will find new motivation in these increased challenges to their managerial abilities. What can local government administrators do to equip themselves to deal more effectively with these difficult new challenges?

Just as the good artisan equips himself with the best tools of his trade, so too can the urban administrator find new tools to work with during the decade of the eighties. New technology can add measureably to the local government administrator's repertoire of tools with which to fight tough new battles in a reduced revenue environment.

EVOLUTION OF NEW PARTNERSHIP

There has been a coming together of new partners during the decade of the seventies that has led to some significant new technologies becoming available to public sector managers.

This new public technology partnership has also led to a heightened awareness of the need for new technology at the local government level; to a strengthened local government capacity to identify technological problems and effect an appropriate solution; and to a growing body of knowledge about how technology may be adapted for local government use. The availability of new technology to meet high-priority local government needs has led to its greater utilization. Direct cost savings, future cost avoidance, and productivity increases have been documented where new technology has been applied. This, in turn, has contributed to increased efficiency and effectiveness of local government service delivery.

This new public technology partnership consists of federal government agencies and their technological laboratories, private industry, universities, nonprofit institutions, public interest groups, and state and local governments.[1] The partnership began forming during the late 1960s as a result of efforts sponsored by such federal government agencies as the National Aeronautics and Space Administration and the National Science Foundation and, to an extent, by the U.S. Department of Housing and Urban Development and the U.S. Department of Transportation. The state and local government efforts were focused and spearheaded by state and local public interest groups, including the International City Management Association, the National League of Cities, the U.S. Conference of Mayors, the National Association of Counties, the National Governor's Conference (now Association), and the National Conference of State Legislatures.

The International City Management Association played a key leadership role when, in early 1970, it developed a Technology Applications Program (TAP) with primary sponsorship by the National Aeronautics and Space Administration. This program led to the separate incorporation in 1971 of Public Technology, Inc. (PTI) as the nonprofit research and develop-

---

[1] James L. Mercer and Ronald J. Philips, Eds., *Public Technology: Key to Improved Government Productivity.* New York: AMACOM, 1981, pp. 1–2.

ment arm of state and local government. This, in effect, created a new state and local government public interest group. Its board of directors at that time consisted of the executive directors of the six public interest groups that formed it. During the decade of the seventies, PTI attempted to be a catalyst to broker the benefits of science and technology to meet the high-priority problems of state and local governments.

PUBLIC TECHNOLOGY, INC.

PTI had its share of growing pains and difficulties during the decade of the seventies, but its accomplishments resulted in greater utilization of science and technology by state and local governments. PTI's major contributions were in the following areas:

• The ability to identify and aggregate, on a national basis, significant and high-priority technology-related needs of local governments.

• The ability to broker those needs to the federal government and to industry in such a manner as to attract federal or private investment in a solution.

• The ability to develop and manage three large national science and technology networks, primarily funded by the National Science Foundation (NSF). These three networks sought to increase the capacity of state and local governments to make greater use of science and technology resources. The three networks are the Urban Consortium for Technology Initiatives for large local governments; the Urban Technology System for medium-size local governments; and the Community Technology Initiatives Program for small local governments.

• The early successes of these networks led NSF to sponsor the formation of a number of other regional, state, and local science and technology networks called "innovation groups." The major benefit of such networks is that they provide local governments with the capacity to understand, identify, and deal with technology.

• A number of accomplishments in developing and transferring software and systems technology to state and local governments (for example, a model for optimally locating fire stations on the basis of response time rather than distance).

• A place for state and local governments to turn for technological information, advice, and possible assistance in problem solving.

• A place for the federal agencies to turn for recommendations in determining how best to structure and conduct research and demonstration programs aimed at assisting the nonfederal public sector.

• A place where industry can learn more about how to adapt or develop products or services for the local government public sector.

As mentioned earlier, PTI has also had its failures. So, too, have many of the other organizations and individuals that have been pioneers in the new technology process. PTI has not been a panacea for state and local government problems. If anything, the state and local expectations about what could be accomplished in a short period of time were probably much too optimistic. The challenge that PTI must face during the eighties is to find ways to motivate and strengthen the public sector/private sector technology partnership. Means must be found to aggregate the fragmented local government market in such a way as to encourage and focus federal and private investment in technology and products for that market.

OTHER EFFORTS

Through their participation in science and technology networks or local government innovation group activities, or sometimes on their own, other organizations made significant contributions to the public sector technology partnership during the 1970s. New centers of specialization in urban technology were established at several institutions and organizations. Examples include Grumman Aerospace Corporation's urban product development group, Oklahoma State University's Center for Local Government Technology, which is a member of NSF's National Innovation Network, the National Association of Counties' Research Foundation, Battelle Memorial Institute's Center for Urban Technology, the Federal Laboratory Consortium for Technology Transfer, and the U.S. Department of Transportation's Technology Sharing Program. The variety of relationships established during the seventies within the overall new public technology partnership and its growing list of achievements will lead to more local government applications of new technologies during the 1980s.

NEW TECHNOLOGIES

The new public technology partnership has resulted in a wide range of hardware/products, software, and systems technologies that can be of benefit to state and local governments during the eighties. It often takes up to ten years to gain acceptance of a technology once it is developed. Therefore, much technology developed during the 1970s should become "fashionable" during the 1980s. There have also been some lessons learned with regard to the process for adapting or transferring various types of technologies to local government use. These will be discussed later in this chapter.

The transfer of technology to local government use has been primarily by the "pull approach." That is, a problem that requires a technological solution is identified and then an appropriate technology is located or developed and transferred to meet the need. This approach is much preferred over the "push approach" in which technology is developed and the developer "pushes" it and hopes it will fit a particular situation.

Hardware/Products

Local government fire service was an area in which a number of hardware or product technologies were introduced or adapted during the 1970s. The fire service had in the past been slow to innovate and use new technologies and techniques but offered promise as a fertile ground for new approaches. PTI was in the forefront of these efforts, with funding assistance from the NASA Technology Utilization Program and what is now the Intergovernmental Science and Public Technology Division of the National Science Foundation.

NPO AUTOMATED FLOW CONTROL SYSTEM

The automated flow control system[2] for a standard fire pumper apparatus enables the local government fire service to control the flow and reach of water at the hose nozzle rather than at the engine. This has increased the safety and effectiveness of fire-fighting operations where this technology has been utilized.

When the fire-fighter nozzleman determines the desired flow rate, a transmitter located between the hose and the nozzle is activated, sending a coded radio signal to a receiver on the pumper truck. The radio signal activates the system, which automatically adjusts the variable flow valve and engine speed, thereby rapidly and accurately providing the selected flow rates. The nozzleman is able to request additional water instantly or to shut off the flow to his line without affecting other lines.

If the fire pumper malfunctions because of excessive pressure, low battery voltage, low oil pressure, or pump cavitation, the automated flow control system warns fire fighters by sounding an alarm and pulsing the water, thereby allowing enough time to correct the problem. Finally, if the automated system itself malfunctions, the fire fighter can immediately revert to manual operation.

Finding a way to give control of the water flow to the nozzleman was one of the top-priority problems defined by 80 local governments in 1970. Grumman Aerospace Corporation approached PTI and convinced it that Grumman possessed the management and technical resources to help design and guide the development of an automated flow control system. The system was subsequently developed and produced by Grumman.

[2] James L. Mercer and Edwin H. Koester, *Public Management Systems.* New York: AMACOM, 1978, pp. 211–214.

Grumman received advice and guidance from a local government User Requirements Committee during the developmental stages.

The system initially sold for about $12,000 to $13,000. It automates two outlets on a standard fire pumper. Cost-effectiveness is realized through:

Better utilization of personnel.
Increased equipment and personnel safety.
Property saved by faster initial response.
Reduced operations and maintenance costs.

In many respects, the program for developing the automated flow control system can be considered a model. The fire service participated in the development of the new product by establishing the requirements, providing input into design and development, and conducting field tests.

However, even with all this positive input into the development of technology, it cannot be considered a commercial success. The total sales of the unit after four years were approximately equal to the expected sales during the first year of production. Many local government administrators and fire chiefs believed the system would improve the cost-effectiveness of the fire service. However, during budget negotiations, the system frequently became subject to trade-offs and cutbacks because of pressures for higher salaries or because inflation raised the cost of other items. The fire-fighters' unions generally did not support and often fought actively against procuring the system, because they viewed it as a means for management to reduce manpower by replacing the pumper operator with the automated system.[3]

Several fire departments in diverse geographic regions purchased and are currently using the automated flow control system. It may be that through those pioneering efforts other local governments will be able to document the advantages of

[3] Warren D. Siemens, *Case Study No. 1: Development of an Automated Flow Control System for the Fire Service.* Mercer and Philips, Eds., *op. cit.,* pp. 176–184.

the system for their own fire service. Through such an approach, this and other new technologies will become more widely used during the 1980s in order to reduce labor intensiveness and costs and to increase safety. Such new utilization can in turn spark developments of other new and needed technologies for local governments.

OTHER FIRE SERVICE DEVELOPMENTS

Through the evolvement of the public technology partnership, several other fire service innovations or technologies were developed during the seventies that are expected to find greater use among local governments during the 1980s. Although many of these new items of equipment can result in improved safety for the fire fighter, the items have, in most cases, also resulted in an improved cost/benefit ratio over current methods in wide use. One of the best known of these developments is the Probeye®[4] Infrared Viewer.[5]

Probeye® was developed by the Hughes Aircraft Company in conjunction with Public Technology, Inc. It is a device that uses thermal radiation to give a clear view of objects, even when there is no light, by projecting images onto a built-in screen. The unit is a product of infrared technology used by the U.S. Department of Defense in weapons systems. Probeye® has the following capabilities for use by the fire service:

1. Detection of first-order fires by the heat radiated or conducted through walls or floors. .
2. Detection and location of fire or smoke victims in dark or smoke-filled environments.
3. Orientation to fire fighters in identifying the physical characteristics of dark or smoke-filled rooms.
4. Identification of residual "hot spots" during clean-up operations.

[4] Probeye® is a registered trademark of the Hughes Aircraft Company.
[5] Mercer and Koester, op. cit., pp. 214–216.

Other local government applications for Probeye® include:

1. Location of potential trouble spots, such as overloaded wires or switches, when making building and electrical inspections.
2. Detection of high-voltage heat buildup during electric utility plant maintenance.
3. Enhancement of vision during police night surveillance operations.

There were some initial problems of locating convenient outlets to recharge the Probeye® Argon bottle, and this created some skepticism about the practicality of the device. However, this problem has been corrected, and a greater use of Probeye® is expected during the 1980s. As a mayor of a small midwestern city remarked after hearing about Probeye®, "If we had had that device in use in our city's fire department, a $100,000 warehouse would have been saved. We thought we had put out a rather minor fire there and after everybody went home, a hot spot rekindled."

An improved fire fighters' breathing system[6]

Under the sponsorship of the National Aeronautics and Space Administration, Scott Aviation Company introduced the first commercially available fire fighter's breathing apparatus on the basis of technology developed for the U.S. Space Program. This was a joint effort between NASA, Scott, several other private firms, and local governments, with Public Technology, Inc. providing the brokerage function.

The result of the development effort was an improved, more reliable, longer-lasting, streamlined, and lighter-weight fire-fighter breathing system. This system was used by a few local governments during the 1970s and its use is expected to increase during the 1980s. The impetus provided by the development of this new technology has spurred other commercial

[6] Warren D. Siemens and J. Tom Smith, *Case Study No. 2: Development of a Firefighters' Breathing System.* Mercer and Philips, Eds., *op. cit.,* pp. 185–190.

developments. Two other closely associated areas of development are new systems for regulating air flow of breathing apparatus and long-duration, re-breather systems for special situations, such as chemical, tunnel, or high-rise fires. These developments should begin to be available for local government fire service use before 1985.

Project fires

Experience with development of the Nozzle Pump Operator mentioned earlier prompted the Grumman Aerospace Corporation to become involved in Project Fires (Fire Fighters' Integrated Response Equipment System). This is a joint effort of the National Aeronautics and Space Administration, the National Fire Prevention and Control Administration, Public Technology, Inc., local governments, and Grumman. The objective of the project is a total redesign of protective clothing for fire fighters, from the boots to the helmet. The basic idea is to develop a totally integrated system similar to that developed for use by astronauts. Preliminary studies showed that such a system would not only better protect the wearer but would also increase the productivity of the fire fighters and ultimately lead to savings for the taxpayers.

Results of this project will have more impact during the 1980s. Resistance to the use of this new system has been expressed and is expected to continue. Most of the resistance is from fire-fighters' unions and stems from unwillingness to part with old traditions. Giving up such traditional symbols as the fire fighter's hat will take a long time.

Other new technologies in the fire, public safety, and emergency communications areas are being developed, and some are expected to come into greater use during the 1980s.

UNDERGROUND UTILITY LOCATOR

Early efforts of the 27 technology agents participating in the National Science Foundation's Urban Technology System revealed a widespread need for a better method of locating underground utility lines. The Urban Technology System is a nationwide program developed and managed by Public Technology, Inc. Its purpose is to apply the benefits of science and technology to the high-priority needs of medium-size local governments across the country.

The purpose of this specific project was to develop an instrument for locating underground utility lines, both metallic and nonmetallic, at a greater depth and with greater accuracy than had been possible with existing equipment.

Through a joint effort of Public Technology, Inc., local governments, and Microwave Associates, Inc., a device based on the concept of downward-looking radar has been developed and is currently being field tested. It is expected to be commercially available during the early part of the decade ahead.

The improved underground pipe and conduit locater system is expected to increase the safety of public utilities and public works crews by pinpointing the locations of buried natural gas and electrical transmission lines. The result will be less inconvenience, less cost to taxpayers, and greater productivity of the public workforce.

AN IMPROVED TECHNOLOGY FOR DETERMINING COLIFORM LEVELS IN WATER[7]

The two accepted methods of detecting and measuring coliform bacteria in public water supplies are often inadequate. One method, multiple-tube fermentation, relies on statistical probability to arrive at a bacterial count. The second method, membrane filter, is more accurate for potable waters since an actual bacterial count is possible. In waters containing solids, this method is unreliable because encapsulated bacteria may be contained in the solids. Both methods require a lengthy in-

---

[7] G. Wade Miller and Arleigh Markham, *Case Study No. 3: "Development of an Improved Technology for Determining Coliform Levels in Water."* Mercer and Philips, Eds., *op. cit.,* pp. 191–200.

cubation period, making the obtaining of same-day results impossible. Therefore, there is a need for a "real-time" alert of bacterial contaminants in water that could affect human health.

A joint technological effort of Atlantic Research Corporation, Public Technology, Inc., local governments, and the federal government has researched a new bacterial testing method known as the reverse phage titer rise reaction (RPTRR). This program was carried out through the Urban Technology System sponsored by the National Science Foundation. It has shown great promise as a technological solution to the need for a faster method to identify bacterial contaminants in water.

Further research and field testing on this technique are continuing. Because it involves public health, it is expected that adoption of this technology will be slow. However, by the late 1980s, it should come into common use by local governments.

OTHER HARDWARE DEVELOPMENTS

There are numerous other technologies already developed or in the planning or design stages that should come into greater use by local governments during the decade ahead. These include the following:

• Various improved methods and materials for patching potholes that were extensively tested by local governments during the seventies.

• Improved approaches to recycling asphalt for streets.

• Improved methods and materials for traffic signs and street striping to improve reliability and wet night reflectivity. A proprietary method using an approach known as molecular grafting exists and the organization that holds the rights to the approach is interested in applying it to local government. What is needed is a catalyst to aggregate the local government market and to assist the developer with some of the front-end costs and with a test and evaluation program. Without such a catalyst, this will be another promising technology that just stays on the shelf.

SOFTWARE/MODELS

In addition to the various hardware or product developments, there are also a number of software packages, approaches, or models that can be used in the public sector to reduce costs, increase productivity, or avoid future costs. Most such approaches are based on economics, management sciences, operations research, industrial engineering, computer and information systems, or similar techniques. Some of the software/modeling approaches developed during the seventies that are expected to find greater utilization during the 1980s are discussed in the following sections.

Fire station locator

The fire station locator is a model for determining the optimal location for a facility. The principles that the model embodies are applicable to the location of many public facilities where proximity to service area is important.

The fire station locator was developed by Public Technology, Inc. It is designed to evaluate and form public policies and to make strategic management decisions about the adequacy of fire station locations. The locator is applicable to both present and planned station locations. Its basic premise is that station locations should be determined on the basis of the time it takes a fire engine to respond to a fire (response time) rather than on arbitrary distance requirements. In this way, jurisdictions have the most fire protection for the least investment.

The fire station locator was developed and tested by a number of local government jurisdictions. Documented savings range from $150,000 to $600,000.

The fire station locator was used in a number of local governments during the 1970s; its use as a local government cost-reduction tool is expected to increase during the 1980s.

Equipment management model

The equipment management model was developed by Public Technology, Inc., with funding assistance from the U.S. Department of Housing and Urban Development. It allows public administrators and equipment managers to decrease the operating and maintenance costs of motorized equipment, to improve efficiency, and to maximize availability of equipment for public use through decreased downtime. Effective monitoring and evaluation of motorized equipment management are the ultimate objectives of the model. The effectiveness of the model depends on whether top management will actually use the computerized reports that it generates. The most accurate reports are useless if they remain unread.

The model is usually implemented by a start-up project team composed of top management, equipment fleet management officials, and various support staff. The output of the model allows administrators and equipment managers to reach objective understanding of inventories, staff levels, and equipment replacement policies that are appropriate to their public sector jurisdictions.

The equipment management model provides detailed information on equipment operating and maintenance characteristics, which enables officials to keep the minimum number of vehicles in service for the maximum amount of time at the minimum cost. Depending on local conditions, the model determines if the equipment fleet size, staff levels, or replacement rates should be less, more, or the same as an organization already has.

Monitoring detailed records of vehicle use by various organizational units within a jurisdiction is a complex task. Effective management analysis of the present and historical costs of fuel, parts, labor, and commercial expenditures usually requires a computerized information system.

The equipment management model was developed and tested by local public officials and equipment managers across the country. The computer programming was performed by local government staff, with Public Technology, Inc. coordination. Most communities involved thus far indicate that the model helps them hold the line on equipment management costs by improving their statistical and cost-accounting procedures.

Street-patching operations decision model

The problem of monitoring streets is highly visible and often becomes a political issue for local elected officials. Yet, little attention has been devoted to evaluating current street maintenance operations and considering new ways of service.

Management must be provided new methods to assess street maintenance operations and to evaluate the impact of alternative modes of operation, new materials, or new equipment. Such new methods will assist local government management in determining where improvements can be made and which alternatives will be the most cost-effective.

The model breaks down street-patching operations into three basic components: labor, materials, and equipment. It allows a jurisdiction to determine and analyze its current street-patching costs and to evaluate the impact of proposed changes. The analysis of current costs and performance suggests ways in which costs can be reduced or performance can be improved.

This model was developed for local governments by Public Technology, Inc. under the auspices of the National Science Foundation's Urban Technology System. It has proved to be an effective tool for those local governments that have used it. Although this model and the equipment management model were developed during the 1970s, their use by a much larger number of local governments is expected during the 1980s.

Resource allocation model for parks management[8]

The Parks and Recreation Bureau of Akron, Ohio, is responsible for maintaining some 70 parks, each two acres or more in size, plus a number of smaller facilities. Determining the optimum mix of maintenance resources (mowers, trucks, tractors, equipment operators, laborers) and the most efficient allocation of those resources has been a continual problem for management. In addition, determining the impact of a proposed

[8] James L. Mercer, "Parks Management/Resource Allocation System." *Ohio Cities and Villages,* November 1978, p. 12.

new park or a change in the level of resources is extremely difficult. Justifying requests for additional resources is equally difficult.

Working through the Urban Technology System, the Akron Technology Agent took a management science approach to the problem. The Technology Agent, working with a professor at Kent State University, mathematically modeled the parks maintenance function, and employed the model to optimally allocate resources, as well as to project the impact of changes in the number of parks, equipment, and manpower.

The model proved valuable to the Akron Parks and Recreation Bureau. The initial runs identified bottlenecks and equipment constraints that had, in some cases, been suspected. These could then be presented in the bureau's budget in quantifiable terms.

Use of the model provides significant savings through more efficient management of the parks maintenance function and elimination of excess resources. Public Technology, Inc. received a major grant from the U.S. Department of Housing and Urban Development to further refine the model and make it available to other local governments. The model's use in parks management is expected to increase during the 1980s. Its generalized features could be applied to a wide variety of resource allocation problems in other local government operating areas.

LESSONS LEARNED

As was mentioned earlier in this chapter, there have been numerous lessons learned during the decade of the 1970s that can be of value in helping local governments adopt new technologies during the 1980s. These "lessons learned" have been grouped into two categories: the role of the individual in science and technology utilization; and technology.[9]

[9] Three additional categories relative to science and technology networks may be found in James L. Mercer and Susan W. Woolston, "The Local Government Science and Technology Network: A National System." Report to the National Science Foundation, April 1979, pp. 27–48.

The role of the individual

It has been shown during the 1970s that the single most important ingredient in successfully applying technology to high-priority local government problems is the role played by key people in the process. Successful utilization of new technology has occurred when individuals have played one or more of the following roles:

- A technically oriented local elected official championed the innovation.
- A politically aware local technical expert championed the innovation.
- An individual from the technology supplier championed the technology through local implementation.
- An individual from the public sector agency spent enough time with the technology to effect a succcessful transfer.

Technology

Several suggestions follow about how best to fit technology to high-priority local government needs:

- The best technology is the appropriate technology.
- Technology should be pulled out for adoption upon user demand, not pushed out at random because there is an abundant supply.
- Technologies that are separable into components are more likely to be accepted.
- The acceptability of a technology depends upon its availability at the time it is needed.
- The "51 percent solution" can be used to define successful technology transfer. That is, if you tried to get 100 percent of a new technology implemented but won 51 percent acceptance, you probably have been successful.
- Technologies that affect only one local government department or group are the easiest to implement (for example, telephone cost control).
- Technologies that affect several departments meet with more resistance (for example, project control system).

- Technologies that require a major capital expenditure on the part of a local government are the most difficult to implement (for example, solar hot water system for a public facility).

9

ESTABLISHING PRIORITIES

IN AN ERA of scarcity, the establishment, evaluation, and systematic review of local government priorities becomes an acute need. Priorities must be considered on a range of issues from the overall goals of the city or county to specific programs or line items in the budget to be eliminated, cut back, or funded as originally conceived. What are some of the methods for establishing priorities? Are the latest techniques, developed in recent years primarily by research organizations, too complex for a practical local government setting? Are they too theoretical and abstract? How does one keep the stronger department heads from dominating priority-setting sessions?

These are among the questions that many city and county managers, chief administrative officers, budget directors, planners, and finance directors ask themselves as costs escalate and revenues become more difficult to obtain.

Many local government situations require systematic approaches to decision making. In the 1980s, as local government circumstances become more complex, decision paths to be taken by public administrators will become more clouded. For example, suppose you, as a public administrator, face one of the following situations:

Situation A. You have recently been designated as City Budget Director. You are to recommend allocations of the needed funds, but the city has no clear method to accomplish this task.

Situation B. As Director of City Planning, you must assist city department heads and division directors in establishing capital improvement program priorities for the next five years. Many have prioritized programs within their own divisions, but not on a department or citywide basis.

Situation C. You are a City Manager. The City Council has requested that you develop a training workshop to assist its members in understanding decision-making techniques they can use to establish priorities among candidate programs to be continued or reduced.

These situations are typical of much of the program and policy planning that takes place in local governments today. Unfortunately, many public decisions must be made in an environment where the goals, constraints, and consequences of possible actions are not precisely known.

In addition to the standard priority-setting methods that have been used by most local governments for years, there are several promising new methods that have developed in recent years. These can help planners, managers, and administrators more clearly and objectively handle the complex problems that arise in an environment of uncertainty. The purpose of this chapter is to describe and discuss three alternative approaches to establishing priorities: Nominal Group Technique, Delphi technique, and Interpretive Structural Modeling (ISM).

TRADITIONAL METHOD

Local governments for years have used the "3 by 5" approach to establishing priorities on everything from overall goals for the city or county to programs, objects, or line items they wish to include in, or exclude from, next year's operating budget or longer-term capital budgets. This method is one in which all items to be considered, ranked, or assigned priorities are written on 3″ × 5″ cards (for example, an addition of a new community center or adding another person to the sanitation crew). Once cards on all items to be considered are prepared, they are sorted by functional groupings such as fire, police, public works, or by programs such as community service, public safety, and the like. At this point, a group meeting at subdepartment or department levels establishes preliminary priorities for the items, projects, and programs by a show of hands or voice vote on each issue. This process moves through successive higher levels within the organization until the chief executive, the elected body, or the citizens make the final decisions as to priorities.

In smaller jurisdictions and in less sophisticated and less toubled times, the 3 by 5 method probably did an adequate job. However, it has several shortcomings:

- It doesn't take into account interdependence between items, programs, projects, and events.
- It is a cumbersome and time-consuming method for handling numerous items and numerous priority-setting alternatives.
- It is often frustrating to those individuals who must agonize over its eventual outcome.
- It doesn't provide built-in mechanisms to deal with the overbearing local official who is going to ramrod his own pet item through regardless of whose toes he must step on in order to do it.

Let us look at some other approaches that can alleviate some of these shortcomings.

PRIORITY SETTING BY EXPERTS

Two of the basic methods that use experts as authorities in establishing priorities are the *sole source method* and the *polling method.* The sole source method employs a single expert to set priorities because of his or her superior knowledge in the field or area. This method is frequently used to predict future economic conditions.

The polling method is an extension of the sole source method. Polling methods use a group of experts rather than just one expert. The polling method has several advantages.[1]

[1] Robert F. Lusch and Gene R. Laczniak, "Future Research for Managers." *Business,* January–February 1979, pp. 41–44.

1. A group of experts can generate and analyze more alternatives.
2. A broader set of facts can be relied on, more opinions can be expressed, and sometimes more estimates of outcome can be developed.
3. Both specialists and generalists can be utilized in areas of high importance to assist in synthesizing facts, refining opinions, and securing estimates of outcome.

Polling methods are excellent means for use by local governments in establishing priorities. The three following techniques are all examples of polling methods.

NOMINAL GROUP TECHNIQUE[2]

The Nominal Group Technique (NGT) is a method of structuring small group meetings in such a way that a systematic outcome can be achieved. NGT was developed in 1968 by Andre Delbecq and Andrew Van de Ven.[3] NGT provides a means to pool individual judgments in situations where uncertainty or disagreement exists concerning the nature of a problem and how it might best be solved. NGT has been used widely by industry and government. It has helped to increase effective citizen participation in government's program planning activities.

NGT is most effective with a small group of people. Groups of five to nine are best. Larger groups can be accommodated if certain minor procedural changes are made in the round-robin recording of ideas portion of the technique (to be discussed in a later section of this chapter). The inventors of NGT recommend that any group larger than 13 should be divided into smaller groups.

[2] James C. Coke and Carl M. Moore, "Guide for Leaders Using the Nominal Group Technique." Columbus, Ohio: Academy for Contemporary Problems, 1979, pp. 1–12. A substantial portion of this section on the Nominal Group Technique was drawn from this guide.
[3] Andre Delbecq, Andrew Van de Ven, et al., *Group Techniques for Program Planning*. Glenview, Ill.: Scott, Foresman and Company, 1975.

The NGT process takes about one and one-half hours if the group is normal-size. It is possible to complete it in just over an hour. An NGT session should not be allowed to last more than three hours.

NGT can be of value in identifying problems, exploring alternative solutions, and establishing priorities. NGT is an especially effective technique to use if there is a danger of verbal dominance by some group members and/or when it is desirable to minimize status difference among group members. NGT is not recommended for simple information exchange, negotiation, or policy setting.

The success of NGT depends upon three essential elements:

1. A carefully thought-out question that will elicit specific responses from the participants.
2. A group of participants who are task-oriented and who possess expertise in the subject matter to be discussed.
3. A group leader who is thoroughly familiar with NGT. This individual must play the role of NGT process facilitator, without offering substantive input or expertise concerning the topic to be discussed.

A variety of preparations should be carefully planned prior to the actual conduct of an NGT session. The same will be true of the Delphi and Interpretive Structural Modeling techniques to be discussed later in this chapter. The four steps to properly prepare for an NGT session are as follows.

Formulating the NGT question

NGT is a single-question technique, so the phrasing of the NGT question is of paramount importance and deserves careful attention. While the utmost simplicity is desirable, the question should be designed to elicit specific responses.

It has been found useful to have several people involved in the preparation of the NGT question. Drafters of the question should agree on the specific objectives of the NGT session and then identify examples of the types of responses they are seeking from the group. With the objectives of the meeting and the examples of results sought in hand, the question can then be composed. If possible, the question should be pilot-tested on a selected group of *nonparticipants* to determine if it evokes the types of responses desired. A well-formulated NGT question might be, What specific barriers do you see to terminating the city's leaf pickup program? A poorly formulated and overly vague question example is, What are the objectives to be achieved and the various steps and substeps necessary to terminate the city's leaf pickup program?

Assembling equipment and supplies

Useful equipment and supplies, such as an easel, flip chart, felt-tip pen, masking tape, and a deck of $3'' \times 5''$ cards, should be assembled before the NGT session. The NGT question should be printed at the top of a sheet of paper, and copies should be made for each participant prior to the session. If this is done, valuable time will not be wasted during the session.

Preparing the meeting room

Ideally, the meeting room should be comfortable, not too warm or cold, and as free as possible from outside interference such as the telephone. It should be possible to tape flip chart sheets on the walls. Tables should be in the shape of a U, with the flip chart easel positioned at the open end.

Training group leaders

If the prospective leaders of the session are inexperienced with NGT, proper training should be arranged beforehand by simulating an NGT session. In the simulation, one can use and test the actual NGT question or a general question. An example of a general question might be, "What difficulties do you anticipate in using the NGT in your department or agency?"

CONDUCTING THE NGT SESSION

The stage for the actual conduct of the NGT session is set by the opening statement. As does the prelude to a play, the opening statement sets the tone for the session. If a group is so large that it is to be divided, the opening statement should be presented in a planning session prior to the beginning of work by each subgroup.

Following are three key elements to include in the opening statement, listed in order of importance to the NGT session:

1. Explain the importance of the task at hand and emphasize that each participant can make a unique contribution.
2. Discuss the overall goal of the NGT session and the intended use of results or output of the session.
3. Describe the four basic steps of the NGT process for those participants who are unfamiliar with NGT.

Four basic steps in conducting the NGT process are silent generation of written ideas; recording of ideas; serial discussion of the ideas; and voting on the ideas.

Step 1: Silent generation of written ideas

This step should be allocated about four to eight minutes' time and should include the following substeps.

Substep 1: Give each participant the NGT question by passing out individual sheets of paper or display the question on a flip chart or an overheard projector. The NGT question should be read aloud. Members of the group should be told to respond to the question by jotting down ideas in phrases or brief sentences because their written lists will not be collected.

Substep 2: Group members should be asked to work silently and independently. Any disruptive behavior and talking should be stopped by the group leader as soon as possible. The leader should set an example by silently writing his or her idea at the same time the group does.

Substep 3: Some participants may ask for clarification regarding the meaning of the NGT question. In responding, the group leader should be careful not to influence members of the group in any particular direction. The degree of abstraction desired can be illustrated, but otherwise participants should be encouraged to respond to the question in a manner that seems most meaningful to them.

Step 2: Recording of ideas

This step is best conducted in four substeps:

Substep 1: The leader should begin by explaining that the objective of this step is to chart the thinking of the group. Each group member, in turn, should be asked to present orally one idea from the list that he or she developed. The idea should be presented only in a brief sentence or phrase. No elaboration or discussion should be offered. This round-robin presentation and recording of ideas should continue until all participants' ideas have been presented.

Substep 2: In this substep, the leader should point out that it is up to each participant to decide if his or her item duplicates any of those presented. The leader should encourage participants to "hitchhike" on the ideas of other group members and to continue to bring up new items, even though they may not have written them down on their list in Step 1. A member can pass any time he or she is called on, but can also reenter the process at any time. During the round robin, the leader should continue to call on members who passed on earlier turns.

Substep 3: The leader should record as rapidly as possible each item mentioned by each group member. Items should be recorded in the group members' own words. They should be sequentially numbered, without abbreviation or condensation. If a person presents a wordy, unwieldy item, he or she should be asked to rephrase the item more simply.

Substep 4: Each filled flip chart sheet should be taped to the wall so that each will be visible to the entire group.

It should be noted that with a large group the length of the list can become burdensome. In such cases, the leader should tell the group in advance that items will be solicited in only two or three rounds. If a list becomes too long, the leader can inform participants that the next round is the last.

Step 3: Serial discussion of the ideas

This step is best conducted in two substeps as follows:

Substep 1: The leader should tell the group that this step is intended to clarify the ideas that have been presented. From the flip charts, the leader reads each item (starting with the first presented) and requests comments from the group on each item. At this time, participants can voice their approval or disagreement regarding any item. Extensive discussion, arguments, or efforts to resolve conflicts are not desirable or necessary since each group member will have an opportunity to vote in Step 4.

The leader should make clear to the group in advance how many minutes are to be devoted to Step 3. Two minutes times the number of items to be discussed is recommended. An alternative, if previous steps have taken longer than anticipated, is to allow the number of minutes until adjournment minus fifteen minutes to be allocated for the final voting.

Substep 2: The leader should encourage the group members to think of the body of items they generated as the property of the entire group. Any participant can comment on any item. It is important that the leader avoid asking the person who contributed an item to clairify that item. Instead, another member should be encouraged to provide clarification, stating, "In my opinion, this item means. . . ."

At this point, a few new items can be added, and small clarifications or editorial changes can be made to existing items. Some reasonable combination of duplicate items is also permitted. But the leader should not permit wholesale combinations of many items into broad categories, because this can destroy the precision of the original items listed.

Step 4: Voting on the ideas

There are two possible voting techniques; ranking and rating. Ranking is the preferred technique because it is the simplest and usually the most effective. Ranking results can be tallied quickly and interpreted easily. The rating technique may be used as an alternative, with each of the seven most important items on a list rated on a one-to-seven scale. The five substeps in the voting process follow.

Substep 1: The leader should give each person five blank

3″ × 5″ cards (seven if the list is long). Participants should select the five (or seven) most important items and write one on
each card. They should also write that item's sequence number
on the card in the upper left-hand corner.

Substep 2: The leader should establish a time limit of four
or five minutes within which the members must select priority
items. Group members should be asked to work silently and not
to rank-order their cards at this point.

Substep 3: This is a rank-ordering process. Once everyone
in the group has completed his or her five or seven cards,
the leader should immediately provide the following instructions:

- Spread your cards out in front of you so you can see all of
  them. Write five (or seven) in the lower right-hand corner
  of the card that you think is more important to you than
  all the others. Underline this number three times and turn
  the card over.
- Decide which of the remaining cards is least important.
  Write one in the lower right-hand corner of this card, underline it three times, and turn the card over.
- Decide which of the remaining cards is most important.
  Write four (or six) in the lower right-hand corner of the
  card, underline it three times, and turn the card over.
- If only five cards are used, select the least important of
  the two remaining cards. Write two in the lower right-
  hand corner, underline it three times, and turn the card
  over.
- If only five cards are used, write three in the lower right-
  hand corner of the last card, underline it three times, and
  turn the card over.
- If seven cards are used, continue similarly until all seven
  cards are numbered.

Substep 4: The leader should shuffle the cards and record
the vote on the flip chart in front of the group. Rankings
should be tallied alongside a column listing of items. For example:

Item 1: 2, 1, 3, 1
Item 2:
Item 3: 5, 3, 5, 5, 4
Item 4: 3, 2
Item 5:

.

.

.

Item N: 3, 5, 1

Substep 5: A discussion of the voting pattern should follow. The item receiving the most consistently high score from the majority of the group is obviously the preferred item. Adding rankings together should be avoided.

USING NGT WITH A LARGE GROUP

As discussed earlier, NGT can be used with large groups, but they should be divided into subgroups. A large group NGT session should begin with a general session at which the leader presents the opening statement. Subgroups of seven to nine persons should then be formed for simultaneous NGT sessions in separate rooms.

After the individual NGT subgroup sessions have been conducted, the subgroup lists should be consolidated with the master list. At least one and one-half hours and preferably two hours should be allowed for the subgroup facilitators to get together and establish a master list. During this time, it is a good idea to occupy the participants elsewhere with a luncheon or panel discussion.

The best way to create a master list is to begin with each subgroup facilitator describing the items that received the strongest support during subgroup voting. Two types of items should emerge from this discussion: duplicate items to be reworded and items unique to one subgroup. The first will require skillful rewording. The second kind can be transferred to the master list almost intact.

The resultant master list will probably contain from 15 to 25 items. As before, these items should be written on flip chart sheets and hung in the large meeting room. The group then meets in plenary session and a facilitator proceeds through NGT Steps 3 and 4.

Summary

Keys to success in using the Nominal Group Technique are proper wording of the NGT question, a group of task-oriented individuals with expertise in the subject being discussed, and, probably most important of all, a group leader who has mastered the NGT process and who will act as a strong facilitator.

DELPHI TECHNIQUE[4]

The Delphi technique is a polling method that can be utilized to attain a consensus from a group of experts without having the experts confront each other in face-to-face debate. It allows participants to learn the opinions of the other experts involved, however.[5]

The Delphi technique overcomes some disadvantages of normal polling methods because it

1. Eliminates the problem of the domineering personality or outspoken individual who takes over the committee process. In a Delphi exercise, a participant fills out each questionnaire by himself and does not know who the other respondents are.
2. Reduces the unwillingness of individuals to take a position on an issue before it is known how the majority feels.

[4] The Delphi technique was developed by Olaf Helmer and Norman Dalkey at the Rand Corporation in 1968–1969. For a discussion of how Delphi can be utilized in deciding between competing or conflicting interests, needs, or activities in a local government setting, see Chapter 2 of James L. Mercer and Edwin Koester, *Public Management Systems*, New York: AMA-COM, 1978.

[5] Lusch and Laczniak, *loc. cit.*

3. Minimizes the difficulty of publicly contradicting individuals in higher positions.
4. Alleviates unwillingness to abandon a position once it is taken publicly.[6]

In the Delphi technique, direct debate among group members is replaced by the interchange of information and opinion through a carefully designed sequence of questionnaires. Group participants are asked not only to give their opinions but the reasons for these opinions. At each successive interrogation, they are given new and refined information in the form of opinion feedback. This information is derived by a computed consensus from the earlier parts of the program. The Delphi process continues until further progress toward a consensus appears to be negligible. The conflicting views are then documented.

The Delphi technique has many applications for reaching consensus under conditions of uncertainty. Establishing priorities is one. To clarify the principles of the Delphi technique, let's consider an example, one that illustrates the procedure that could be followed in seeking an answer to a fairly narrow question.

Example: Choosing a number by Delphi

Consider a common situation that is likely to arise in most local governments during the 1980s. How much should we cut back the parks maintenance budget? What will the resultant budget, N, for this function be after our necessary cutback?

We would first gather a group of experts on the topic to be discussed, much as we would do if we were going to use the Nominal Group Technique. One major difference is that, depending on the applications, we could use a computer terminal to act as a real-time bookkeeper for the session. This is called "Delphi conferencing." The computer would maintain an up-

[6] G. Weltz, "Problems of Selecting Experts for Delphi Exercises." *Academy of Management Journal,* March 1972, pp. 121–124.

to-the-minute record of the session. A complete summary of where the session stands at any given moment would be available to the terminal operator.

In our parks maintenance question, we would proceed as follows (without using the computer):

1. We would ask each expert to give an independent estimate of N (the dollar amount to be budgeted for next year for the parks maintenance function). To preserve anonymity, this could be done by writing estimates on $3'' \times 5''$ cards.

2. We would then arrange the responses from the individual participants in order of magnitude and determine the quartiles, $Q1$ containing the lowest group of estimates, M containing one-half of the median group of estimates, and $Q3$ containing three-fourths of the estimates. We would make certain that one-fourth of the estimates fell in $Q1$, one-half in M, three-fourths in $Q3$, and all in N. If we had eleven participants, the N line might look like this.

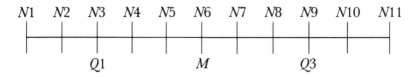

3. We would then communicate the values of $Q1$ (for example, $1 million), M ($1.5 million), and $Q3$ ($2 million) to each respondent. We would ask him to reconsider his previous estimate. If his estimate (old or revised) lies outside the interquartile range ($Q1$, $Q3$), he would be asked to state briefly the reasons, in his opinion, that the answer should be lower (or higher) than the 75 percent majority opinion experienced on the first round.

4. We would communicate the results of this second round (which as a rule will be less dispersed than the first) to the respondent in summary form, including the new quartiles and median. In addition, we would document the reasons the experts gave in Round 2 for raising or lowering the values (as collated and edited, these reasons would, of course, preserve the anonymity of the respondents).

5. We would then ask the experts to consider the new estimates and the arguments offered for them and to give them the weight they think they deserve. In light of this new information, we would ask them to revise their previous estimates. Again, if the revised estimates fall outside the second range, we would ask each respondent to state briefly why he found unconvincing the argument that might have drawn his estimate toward the median.

6. Finally, in the fourth round, we would submit both quartiles of the third distribution of responses and the counterarguments elicited in Round 3 to the respondents and encourage them to make one last revision of their estimates. The median of these Round 4 responses could then be taken as representing the group's position as to what N, the budget for the park's maintenance function, should be.[7]

Summary

In comparison with other processes for reaching consensus under conditions of uncertainty, several important observations may be made regarding the Delphi technique:

- Face-to-face discussions are not as efficient as more formalized communications.
- Estimates are improved and made more accurate with each iteration.
- Accuracy improves when estimates of range as well as the single points are requested and supplied.

Delphi provides a technique that is particularly suited to investigating and establishing priorities for many problems with a high social and political content. Because it can estimate the consequences of alternative actions, thus substituting for more conventional models, Delphi potentially introduces a more structured systems approach into a range of problem solving where it is difficult to formulate precise models.

[7] E. S. Quade and W. I. Boucher, Eds., *Systems Analysis and Policy Planning: Applications in Defense.* New York: American Elsevier Publishing Co., 1968, pp. 334–335.

INTERPRETIVE STRUCTURAL MODELING

Interpretive Structural Modeling (ISM) is a technique to help people think and communicate more effectively about complex issues. It is implemented in such a way that people are responsible for making subjective judgments, while a computer is used for bookkeeping and for displaying the results and implications of human decision making. ISM was developed by the Battelle Memorial Institute's Columbus Laboratories and has been successfully implemented numerous times in state and local government environments.

The fundamental concept of ISM involves the delineation of relationships existing between a set of issue statements (elements) that may reflect objectives, goals, activities, factors, or variables identified within the context of a problem situation.

The process involves defining an *issue context* or a statement of general concern. For example, "What factors are important for consideration in a land-use suitability analysis for residential development?" An *element set* is subsequently identified, reflecting the context of the issue statement, in this case, a set of relevant data variables attracting or restricting residential development. A *relational statement* is constructed in the form of a single clause expressing a meaningful transitive relationship among the elements. For example, "Is variable A a stronger constraint to residential development than variable B?" The primary product is a *digraph,* or representation of the relative structure established by the user (in this example, a structured ranking of the elements most constraining to development).

A finalized *structural model* may then be derived after careful examination and possible revision of the original digraph and its components, or from a reiteration of the entire process. By using various combinations of elements and relationships, the results can be priorities, organization charts, data interaction diagrams, support structures, objective trees, relevant trees, or whatever description is meaningful to the participants. The only operational limitation is that the nature of the relationship must be transitive, meaning that it must be possible to infer the relationship from some elements to others through an intermediary element or elements.

USE OF ISM IN LOUISIANA: A CASE STUDY[8]

ISM has been applied in Louisiana (1) for ranking and structuring regional goals in six of the eight areawide planning districts; (2) as a teaching aid for an urban and regional planning course in the Urban Studies Institute, University of New Orleans, to relate energy resource conservation programs; (3) for ranking and structuring transportation goals for a parish area planning commission; and (4) for ranking constraints to development in suitability modeling for the Coastal Zone Management Program. ISM has also been used as an aid to citizen involvement in some of these projects and for demonstrations to professional groups.

Planning district pilot projects

The first use of ISM in Louisiana has been the most extensive application to date. The Louisiana Commission on Intergovernmental Relations (IGR), now the State Department of Community and Urban Affairs (DCUA), was designated as the administrator of the HUD 701 planning program in 1974. At that time, the state had no clear direction for allocating monies. All alternatives for remedying this inadequacy made it evident that goals and objectives on which to base priority funding were needed. In recognizing the dual need for the clear identification of goals and for citizen participation, IGR began searching for a systematic planning process. Working with Battelle, the commission, after review of alternatives, selected the Decision Structuring Process. The Decision Structuring Process (DSP) was selected because it satisfied the following criteria:

[8] Dewitt H. Braud, Jr. and Donna M. Irvin, Louisiana Commission on Intergovernmental Relations, Baton Rouge, Louisiana, and Kazuhiko Kawamura, Battelle Columbus Laboratories, Columbus, Ohio. Paper presented at the Seventh Annual Pittsburgh Conference on Modeling and Simulation, Pittsburgh, April 1976.

- Can interface with many segments of the population, urban and rural.
- Can be readily grasped and easy to use.
- Can be presented within a short time period at a workshop.
- Can achieve results within several months to one year.
- Has been previously tested and found usable by a four- or five-person staff.
- Is relatively inexpensive to implement.

A pilot district was selected to implement DSP in an initial test application (Kisatchie-Delta Regional Planning and Development District in Alexandria, Louisiana). A 12-member citizen committee was organized.

ISM was chosen as the technique for structuring goals and objectives during the pilot project. A citizens' committee was formed of representative citizens of the area. The citizens were adequately briefed prior to their first work session concerning the purpose of the committee and the methodology to be employed. The district composed an issue statement. This served as a focal point for the committee and was phrased as follows: "What do you think are important community and regional needs?"

The first meeting took the citizens' group into a needs assessment. The Nominal Group Technique (NGT) was used in the needs assessment.

The next step required a translation of the needs into goals. The district staff was requested to clarify the goals and objectives from the NGT session by reducing redundancies and discarding any goals that could not be affected by the 701 process. From this information, a set of 20 goals and objectives was constructed to present to the citizens.

The citizens' group was assembled for the second time to rank the 20 goals with the aid of ISM. They were told to make any changes they desired. After the goals were resolved to the satisfaction of everyone, the element set was systematically ranked according to priority, using the relational phrase "more important than." All questions during the process compared the relative degree of importance of the elements until all possible element combinations had been considered.

Although citizen input was obtained for identifying and ranking planning-related goals, it was agreed that an additional ISM exercise was needed to determine a support hierarchy that would supply valuable information regarding the significance of goals, that is, a determination of how the achievement of certain goals would affect the achievement of others. Since the determination of this support relationship depended heavily on a certain level of knowledge regarding the planning aspect of the identified goals, it was decided to use only the district planning staff. The staff structured the goals, using the support relationship "help achieve."

Subsequent to the construction and analysis of goals and objectives, the Kisatchie-Delta staff proceeded to identify 23 planning alternatives specifically selected to satisfy the goals and objectives. Limitations in the choice of alternatives were imposed by restrictions in the HUD program.

The first step in the evaluation of alternatives involved the determination of those capable of achieving the largest number of high-priority goals. This approach was taken for the following reasons:

- Some goals are multifaceted and cannot be achieved with the application of only one program.
- Some goals are requisite to or will substantially aid the accomplishment of others.
- Some alternatives will apply to a broad range of goals.

In view of this complex situation, the planning staff was asked to carefully determine the extent of relationship of each alternative to each goal. The staff dealt with this problem by grading the degree to which each alternative would satisfy each goal on the basis of a 0 to 3 scale (0, least; 3, greatest). The result was a 20 × 23 matrix used to rank alternatives.

Although this phase of the evaluation was highly subjective, it was necessary that the Kisatchie-Delta planning staff maintain a consistent approach in grading alternatives. In doing this, the staff used reference criteria as a basis for their judgments. These criteria consisted of the scope and purpose of planning projects and their utility for purposes other than that primarily designated.

The next procedure assigned weights to each goal on the basis of its position in the two goals structures. First, weights, designated R, were assigned to each goal on the priority structure on the basis of importance. Then, weights, S, were assigned to each goal on the support structure according to the level each was in. Elements at the top were considered least supportive and thus given lower weights. The two weight scales were then made equivalent by a correction factor applied to the support weight, and the two weights for each goal were combined to give a final weight. The priority weight was given twice the significance when combined.

The results of the matrix of alternatives versus goals and the final weights obtained for each goal were used in a linear scoring procedure to obtain a relative rank for each alternative since it was desirable to know which alternatives were most useful. In the matrix, each alternative, A_i, was evaluated according to its ability to achieve each goal, G_j, and resulted in a rating, r_{ij}. Using the relative weights, w_j, calculated for each goal, the alternatives were ordered according to the scores, s_i, obtained from

$$S_i = {}_j w_j \times r_{ij}$$

Since this is a subjective ranking procedure, precise mathematical accuracy is not critical. The desired result is an overall indication of relative levels of importance in planning alternatives.

The experience of the pilot project was instrumental in smoothing out and improving implementation of the methodology on a statewide basis. Several recommendations were made to effect procedural changes, and many suggestions helped improve the application of the techniques so as to avoid difficulties encountered in the pilot study. The grouped alternatives were used in making decisions for funding planning projects by serving as a major indicator of the direction these projects should take.

SUBSEQUENT ISM APPLICATIONS

The DSP methodology was implemented in five additional planning districts following the success of the pilot project. Each district applied a slightly different variation of the methodology to accommodate its area, and recommendations resulting from the pilot project were incorporated into this phase.

A similar application of ISM as that used in the pilot project was employed by the Rapides Area Planning Commission to interrelate transportation goals. This project resulted in a more detailed support structure from which considerable inferences can be made.

The Coastal Zone Program in Louisiana has used ISM to rank environmental and human-related factors pertaining to the suitability of land for specific uses, such as agricultural, residential, and industrial. These rankings were then applied in suitability modeling to derive maps of areas favorable for development according to applied criteria. Since variables are interrelated and cannot be considered in isolation, a possible future application of ISM may be to determine the pattern of data variable influence. If this could be done, then planners should be able to outline patterns of reaction resulting when environmental parameters are affected by disturbances from human activities.

10

PERSONNEL AND
PERSONNEL MANAGEMENT

WHAT EFFECTS will reduced revenues have on local government personnel during the 1980s? What new approaches to personnel management must local government managers pursue during the next decade? What special types of personnel backgrounds and skills must local governments seek in order to adequately handle new technologies and complex decisions in an environment with less resources? These are the questions this chapter will address.

It has been said that if you as a manager take care of your personnel problems first, most of your other problems will go away. This statement has considerable validity since most of the work of cities and counties is carried out by and through people. *People* costs make up more than 80 percent of the typical local government budget. *People* deliver services and take care of day-to-day complaints and problems. *People* can find new ways to be more productive, or not, depending on how they are trained and motivated. The tremendous challenge to the local government administrator of the eighties will be how to reduce the cost and increase the efficiency of government and yet continue to maintain a harmonious and highly motivated local government workforce.

BACKGROUND OF PUBLIC ADMINISTRATION

Traditionally, local government officials trained themselves or moved up through the ranks of fire, police, or public works until they reached the top spot. Some have migrated over from the private sector and some have had careers in the military. Most of the early city managers were civil engineers, because the city manager position required a knowledge of streets and sewer and water lines and facilities.

Over the past 25 to 30 years, professional education opportunities expanded, and today most city and county managers hold one or more degrees in public administration. Many city and county department heads also have degrees in public administration or in their functional specialty area, such as city planning.

There is little doubt that the management of most cities and counties is in the hands of a highly professional, well-educated, and dedicated group of individuals. The problem is that managing with reduced revenue has not been something that most local government administrators have had to face before. Their education and experiences have not prepared them to deal with this situation. Few have the time to return to school, so much trial and error is inevitable. There will be successes and also failures. Being the first to try a new idea, especially if its chances of success are uncertain, is not always inviting when you're working in the fishbowl environment of public service. Coping adequately with many of the problems and opportunities of the eighties, however, will require experimentation and risk taking. The key is to find ways to minimize risks and maximize opportunities and positive results.

During the 1970s, a new breed of public administrators arrived on the local government scene in response to a new emphasis on productivity improvement. The earliest manifestation was probably the industrial engineer (IE). Industrial engineers had succeeded in increasing efficiency and cutting costs in the private sector. Quite naturally, when the public sector wished to do the same, it turned to industrial engineers who had been successful in the private sector. Frequently, local governments that created this position placed the IE in a staff position to the top administrator or in a budget or management improvement department. Usually, industrial engineers performed in a staff capacity with responsibility for carrying out a broad range of cost-reduction and productivity-improvement projects.

In some cities and counties, an individual with a background in management systems was retained. Frequently, both capabilities were contracted for from outside consulting firms. In rare instances, the IE or Systems Engineer/Analyst was brought into the organization as, or developed into, a line operating manager. Some stayed in the public service. Others became consultants to public sector organizations. Some returned to the private sector. Although individual jurisdictions benefited and some cross-fertilization of successes occurred among jurisdictions, there has been no really widespread, long-term use of large numbers of industrial engineers by cities and counties.

In the early 1970s, numerous federally sponsored programs were initiated to bring scientists, technologists, engineers, systems analysts, and operations research personnel into local governments, at least on a temporary basis. The basic premise of these programs was that the introduction of new technologies could help reduce current costs, avoid future costs, and improve the productivity of local government operations. One of the largest and most successful of these programs, the Urban Technology System (UTS), is described in Chapter 8.

The basic methodology of UTS is to place scientists, engineers, or systems analysts at the assistant city or county manager level and to give them backup support from a research and development organization. They then identify local government problems that have a technological component and act as a broker to seek out and implement solutions. Many programs such as UTS have now been started. By the end of the 1970s, more local governments took advantage of better scientific and technical advice in their managerial decision making through participation in local government technology networks.

This chapter will discuss two aspects of personnel administration in local government: What types of personnel will be required to manage and operate the local governments of the 1980s; and what changes will be likely to occur in the local government personnel function *per se* during the decade ahead?

MANAGERS FOR THE 1980s

Most of the top administrators in local governments during the 1970s will undoubtedly continue their roles into the 1980s. It is likely, however, that new managerial styles and techniques will be required of these administrators as they attempt to deal with the cost/revenue squeeze.

The Simon Legree-type sweatshop manager of the early 1900s has never been acceptable in most local government settings. The Boss Tweed-type mayor and chief executive of the early part of this century is definitely not acceptable in today's local governments. During the past two decades, the scientific manager who was a product of the Frederick W. Taylor school of scientific management has been criticized. In recent years, there has been a shift toward a more humanistic approach to local government personnel management. Research by Dr. Rensis Likert, retired director of the University of Michigan's Institute for Social Research, and others has proved that managers who encourage participation in decision making by all levels of employees within an organization are the most successful managers.

There is a definite trend for the more humanistic and participative approach to management to replace the autocratic and impersonal efficiency expert approach to management in local, state, and federal governments. People can no longer be considered as mere inputs into the production process. Participative approaches to management in which everyone comments on decisions before they are made has replaced the more scientific approach. Full-blown participative management, where inputs are sought from many sources before decisions are reached, can be time consuming, frustrating, and costly in both time and effort. It seems a less productive approach to management, but when decisions are made, their implementation is usually more easily accepted by employees because they participated in making the decision. The results, therefore, may be more effective than those reached by other managerial approaches.

Has the pendulum been allowed to swing too far in this direction? Have laissez-faire approaches replaced true participative management? Some managers who believe they are practicing participative management have actually abdicated their positions as managers, and a country club organizational atmosphere prevails. Perhaps what will be regained during the 1980s is a reasonable compromise between the two schools of scientific management and participative management. Such an approach would combine the benefits of individual input into the decision-making process, with the use of more efficient techniques to increase productivity and more economical use of resources. Achieving such a compromise will be one of the local government manager's challenges for the 1980s.

In order to be effective in this approach, the local government administrator of the eighties will need to call on many resources and experts, including:

- Individuals and organizations knowledgeable about technology and its benefits.
- Individuals and organizations knowledgeable about how to involve people in decision making and how to keep them motivated.
- The administrator's own knowledge of how to use and integrate more efficient and effective approaches to management.

Specific sources of assistance to the administrator include:

City or county staff
Outside consultants
Independent research and development organizations

State and regional governments (multistate and substate)
Federal government agencies and their laboratories
Neighborhood and citizen organizations
Other local governments
Associations of cities and counties
Professional membership organizations
Private firms and their associations
Private individuals
Foundations
Colleges, universities, and technical schools (public and
   private)

Although the possibilities for outside technical assistance to cities and counties are virtually limitless, it should be recognized that some sources are of higher quality and/or are more timely than others. Some assistance is more manageable than others, and some is more costly. The old adage that "you get what you pay for" has a lot of credence, and one well-informed consultant may be worth two inexperienced volunteers.

The basic objective is to establish an approach where someone—a person, a group, or an organization—can devote a sufficient amount of time learning to understand the local government organization, can exhibit the perspective and courage to define problems or areas of opportunity, and can follow through to implementation of appropriate and acceptable solutions. By and large, the top administrator and department heads don't have the time to devote to this effort. Also, there are problems of perspective, tradition, and background. Most public administration programs do not train students in science and technology, for example. If a staff member has been with the city or county for a long period of time, his or her perspectives on potential areas for cutback or efficiency improvement may have become stale. People have a tendency to be loyal to whatever has worked before. Many seasoned staff members will avoid taking on controversial or high-risk changes or innovations for fear of "bucking" long-standing traditions. A new staff member or an outsider usually doesn't have such problems and can provide a fresh perspective.

LOCAL GOVERNMENT PERSONNEL FUNCTIONS
IN THE 1980s

Local government personnel may be the function that will undergo the most dramatic changes during the decade ahead. With more women and minorities entering the workforce, with cutback management becoming a reality, and with the workforce more highly educated and demanding better training and opportunities to be involved in decisions, increasing pressure will be placed on the personnel function. Is the local government personnel department equipped to handle these new challenges?

A recent survey of local, state, and federal government agencies was sponsored by the U.S. Office of Personnel Management (OPM) and the Council of State Governments (CSG). Its conclusions were that personnel departments in local, state, and federal governments lack comprehensive programs to recruit minority and women applicants and that they do not have adequate training programs.[1] These conclusions, of course, apply mostly to the many small local governments. Most medium-size and large local governments are better equipped and staffed, but they still need management attention in the decade ahead.

During the past two decades, state and local government employment has increased dramatically. Currently, there are over four times more state and local government employees than there are federal government employees. Proposition 13 and similar measures across the country have focused more public attention on the large number of local government employees. The belief of many taxpayers that they are not getting their money's worth from the local government workforce has created tension at local government levels. Some local government employees are leaving the workforce voluntarily because of it. Others are being forced to leave because of service or

---

[1] "Local Personnel Departments Lack Comprehensive Programs." *Public Administration Times,* May 15, 1980, p. 2.

budget reductions. Some are remaining and a portion of these are resorting to political means or unionization to try to maintain adequate pay and working conditions. Morale of the workforce is often low, creating problems for local government administrations and personnel departments.[2]

Because of the high labor-intensiveness of most local government functions, the effective management of personnel is particularly essential to a productive operation. In managing personnel, however, local government administrators are often hindered by factors beyond their control. These include economic conditions, politics, and legal factors. The cost of employing personnel is a major deterrent to adding more policemen to fight rising crime, adding additional fire fighters, and so on. There are also administrative constraints that limit the local government administrator's ability to hire, train, assign, motivate, and dismiss employees. Many local government personnel systems overlap with state systems. Innovative or flexible operation of personnel programs are often thwarted by unions, patronage, and merit or civil service systems. All these can deter effective personnel management.

If local government officials in the 1980s are to be accountable for results in a more stringent fiscal environment, they must have a personnel system that is responsive and conducive to a high level of performance by the public workforce. Such personnel systems must:

- Be structured in such a manner that both political and economic factors are considered.
- Have compensation plans that are closely attuned to the fiscal constraints on local government.
- Deal practically with the fact that workers can engage in job actions that can disrupt public services.
- Assure internal consistency and compatibility among key

[2] "Improving Management of the Public Work Force: The Challenge to State and Local Government." Summary of a statement by the Research and Policy Committee of the Committee for Economic Development, New York, November 1978, pp. 11–13.

components of the personnel system including the following:

1. Improved employee recruitment and selection techniques, including those related to minorities and women.
2. Systematic and continually updated job classification and pay plans.
3. Merit systems that take into account the realities of collective bargaining.
4. Means to assure that collective bargaining is attuned to the overriding priority of preserving the merit system.
5. Means to assure that collective bargaining is closely linked with the realities of managing public sector agencies.[3]

A good local government personnel system must also be sensitive to the dramatic changes taking place in the characteristics and desires of employees, the kinds of employees in the workforce (and their educational and work backgrounds), and the new techniques and skills required in the day-to-day management of the public workforce. This new generation of workers, which will be better educated and include more minorities and women, will need different training programs and different employee relations programs than local governments have traditionally provided.

Two overall goals that should be established for any good local government personnel system are emphasis on effective and efficient public service, and fair treatment of public employees. Many factors will affect achievement of these goals. Some have been cited previously. Others are

- A personnel policy that clearly delineates the different roles of the policy makers, professional managers, and other employees.
- Personnel procedures and practices based on merit that

[3] *Ibid.,* pp. 14–16.

protect employee rights but are supportive of management.

- Development of managerial capability as a key to effective personnel management.
- Structuring of collective bargaining (where appropriate) that takes into account the political nature of local government.
- Special attention to, and experimentation with, different ways local government individual functions can be performed to improve employee performance, job satisfaction, and personal development.[4]

During the past two decades, goals and objectives of many local governments have become less clear as the size and complexity of the organization increased and as programs proliferated. Because of a need to manage with less during the 1980s, there will be a sharper focus placed on the management of the local government workforce. Goals and objectives in the 1980s are expected to include the following:

A revitalization of the merit principle. Ability and performance should be the criteria for recruiting, selecting, assigning, promoting, and compensating local government employees. Over the past two decades, too much reliance has been placed on seniority as a reason for promoting and compensating people in local government. Such an approach often overlooks the people most qualified for positions. During the 1980s, more local governments will restructure their personnel functions and related systems to:

1. Use personnel administration techniques that assure the best people possible are available for each assignment. A growing trend is for local governments to make greater use of outside executive search firms and personnel agencies to assure the widest possible coverage and to save time. Many personnel activities in the 1980s will include improved testing, evaluations, and training programs for employees or prospective em-

---

[4] *Ibid.*

ployees and a management-by-objectives system in which all levels of employees know and participate in the establishment of standards and goals that their actual performance will be measured against.

2. Assure that collective bargaining arrangements, when appropriate, do not restrict management from using employees' skills and potential to the fullest.

3. Assure that discrimination because of race, sex, national origin, or cultural background does not prevent talented people from being hired and promoted.

Restoration of the authority of managers to manage. Too many public sector managers are expected to manage efficiently and effectively, but laws and agreements that have accumulated through the years have eroded their managerial authority. Because of restrictive policies and other imposed constraints, many managers are truly constrained in their activities; nevertheless, they are blamed for failure to manage effectively.

During the 1980s, there will be a restoration of the local government manager's *authority* to manage. Managers must be given the authority and resources to accomplish established objectives. They should then be held accountable for results. The multitudinous array of personnel restrictions that have come about during the past two decades often prevent local government managers from doing a good job and, in some instances, provide excuses for poor performance. Authority to manage is crucial to an efficient and effective local government operation.

Protection of the rights of employees. During the 1980s, with an increase in cutback management, there will be a sharpened need to protect local government employees from capricious political abuse and arbitrary action by bureaucrats. There are several aspects of this goal:

1. Protection of the rights of individuals in employment.

2. Respect for the interests of individuals.

3. Effective and efficient government is best provided by employees who are secure in the knowledge that their performance will be judged on how well they serve the public and that

they, as individuals, will be treated with fairness and dignity.

Enhancement of personal performance, development, and job satis-faction. During the 1980s, more emphasis in local government personnel policy will be placed on these factors:

1. Enhanced performance of employees at all levels.

2. Training and development of individual employee capabilities.

3. Improved quality of working life.

During the past two decades, many otherwise highly motivated local government employees have been hampered and frustrated by a host of impediments to doing a good job. These include bureaucratic barriers, a lack of clearly established objectives, and little or no feedback on their performance. Performance feedback is important for motivating employees. Other negative factors include inept supervision that wastes employees' time and talent. Local government employees represent a wealth of talent that should have the room and the encouragement to grow and develop to the fullest extent possible. Job situations need to be created that are conducive to and supportive of productive work and simultaneously are satisfying and fulfilling to employees.[5]

Some additional practical strategies local governments can employ in their search for an efficient and effective personnel management system, as described in this chapter, are the following:

Disclosure. Local governments should make known to employees and the public that because of the burden of personnel costs on the budget, the operating budget cannot be reduced without cutting back personnel. To maintain service levels, this means more productivity and hard stands by management in collective bargaining.

Collective bargaining. Local governments should consider hiring good professional negotiators on the grounds that their short-term costs will be offset by long-term savings to the jurisdiction. Negotiators should ask for measurable productivity in-

---

[5] Ibid., pp. 16–18. Much of this section was drawn from this report.

creases in return for concessions and compromises in pay and benefits.

Personnel mobility. Local government managers should encourage systems that focus on mobility, not rigidity. Exchanges of personnel through the provisions of the Intergovernmental Personnel Act can bring new ideas into local governments and provide regular employees with new and challenging temporary assignments at other levels of government. This can motivate them and also give them intergovernmental relations expertise. Innovative arrangements for temporary personnel exchanges with private sector firms are also valuable.

Incentives and penalties. Human behavior is motivated by the prospect of both incentives and penalties. These should be clearly evident in a well-structured personnel management system. Management-by-objectives programs enable performance to be assessed more clearly by both employee and supervisor. Local governments should make full use of nonfinancial motivators such as personal achievement awards, time-off bonuses, and community recognition of productivity improvements.

Importance of professional personnel management. In a cutback environment, it is tempting to eliminate "staff" positions such as personnel. Such moves fail to recognize that the personnel function may be even more important in times of financial stress. More attention than ever must be placed on a sound position classification and pay plan, which the public and the policy makers can review continually and which can be the basis for participation in personnel and budgetary decisions. Opportunities for automation of functions or consolidation of positions are more evident when clear information is available about functions and costs of all local government positions. A good personnel manager can keep administrators advised of long-term fiscal impacts of pensions and benefit plans.

Circumstances in the 1980s will force many local governments to reexamine the goals and objectives of their personnel management systems. Most local governments have not developed comprehensive personnel programs that include all or even many of the elements discussed in this chapter. Developing such systems with incentives for productivity improvement will be another challenging opportunity for local government administrators in the 1980s.

11

COLLABORATIVE STRATEGIES WITH
THE PRIVATE SECTOR

Private sector/public sector collaborative efforts are under way across America as never before. Many of the more current efforts have resulted from taxpayer revolts, such as California's Proposition 13 and its resultant backwash, as well as from a desire by business and government leaders to prevent similar situations from occurring in their communities. Many local government administrators and private sector businessmen fear that financial crises, such as those experienced by New York and Cleveland, could happen in their city or county. The private sector sees its livelihood intertwined with good local government; local government sees its viability tied to a prosperous private business base within its jurisdiction. Many public/private partnerships have been ongoing for a number of years. They offer some excellent examples of mutually rewarding experiences.

The purpose of this chapter is to describe and discuss several promising private/public collaborative efforts that have been developed during the seventies and to project the extension of these and other efforts into the eighties.

There are three basic types of public/private collaborative efforts: voluntary efforts by private firms, joint business ventures, and contracting out of public activities and functions to private firms (privatization). Each of these will be discussed in greater detail in the following sections.

VOLUNTARY EFFORTS

Voluntary public/private collaborative efforts have been under way for many years. On the part of the private firm, most of these efforts stem from the firm's public service motive. This motive is to a large degree the result of private corporate leadership's desire to have a high-quality community within which its employees can live and work, and where business leaders can be confident that the tax dollars the firm pays are being used wisely. Lloyd B. Dennis, Director of Public Affairs and Chairman of the Social Policy Committee of the United California Bank, recently wrote:

> The economic breakdown of several of our major cities is due in large measure to a failing in the private as well as the public sectors of the very cities that are hurting the most. It is a failure to communicate and a failure to accept responsibility. It is a failure to see the long-range benefits to both the private and public sectors in their working together toward the economic strength and viability of the communities in which they work and live.[1]

Loaned executive programs

Dennis is a pioneer in public/private partnerships in California. His efforts began in 1976 in the wake of New York City's financial crisis. After discussions with numerous public and private officials throughout California, United California Bank (UCB) decided to act as the catalyst to bring about a new public/private partnership. The purpose of this new partnership was to produce results beneficial to the long-term economic health of the cities and counties involved.

UCB developed an urban team approach made up of task forces of professionals in economics, banking, urban planning, accounting, computer technology, political science, and per-

---

[1] Lloyd B. Dennis, "Public/Private Partnerships: Watchwords for the 1980s." *Western City*, February 1979, pp. 16–17 and 24.

sonnel administration. These task forces were to offer free consulting services to cities in the 50,000 and under population range. The plan sought to select cities where good rapport and harmony existed between the elected City Council, the appointed City Manager, and the city's Chief Financial Officer. The purpose was to address economic and financial difficulties, not internal political problems. The idea, too, was for the task forces to have high visibility with city staff and department heads to achieve a lasting image of public/private cooperation.

Two cities selected for the pilot program were Montebello in southern California and Saratoga in northern California. The areas of financial management, planning, and productivity improvement were initially selected for concentration by the task forces. The two teams consisted of more than forty volunteers, two full-time professionals, and one paid public sector consultant.

The three major stages of this voluntary program were (1) identification of problems and opportunities, (2) development of solutions, and (3) preparation of extensive written documents that were presented to city executives.

Work productivity programs were developed, and city employees were taught how to identify and correct inefficiencies. Based on the success of the Montebello and Saratoga efforts, in 1978 the program was repeated in Montclair and Union City. At this point, cities actively sought the service, which is an indication of its value in the two pilot cities.

Common threads uncovered in the four cities were difficulties in linking annual spending to long-term service objectives; and the need to develop a stronger commercial and industrial tax base for planned expansion.

One key to the success of this model program in California was that mutual sensitivity, trust, and understanding were fostered by the task force members and by the management and employees of the cities.

What have been the longer-term results of this pilot program in California?

Under the leadership of a Boston bank, a similar program

is being adapted to the needs of 11 New England cities in the small to medium-size category.

In Seattle, a bank is developing a small pilot effort to assist cities in the Puget Sound area.

The government of the Philippines has discussed the possibility of a similar program there.

The California Roundtable, an organization of presidents and chairmen of the state's major corporations, created a state-wide Loaned Executive Program. This program was expanded to include assistance to counties, water and school districts, public libraries, and other governmental units with financial management and planning needs.[2]

There are many voluntary programs similar to that of UCB in other areas of the country. The nearly broke city of Niagara Falls, New York, was assisted back to a sound financial footing within a year by a group of local businessmen who formed the City Management Counsel. Similarly, top business leaders in Oakland, California, are offering free consulting to their city in the areas of insurance, payroll, and data processing. The late mayor of San Francisco, George Moscone, created a Committee for San Francisco to review the management of city departments and to make results-oriented suggestions for improving service delivery in a reduced revenue environment. Mayor Feinstein has further supported and encouraged this effort.[3]

In Pittsburgh, Pennsylvania, the chief executive officers of the twelve largest corporations headquartered there formed, in 1976, the Committee for Progress in Allegheny County (Com-PAC). The key to this private sector response was a request from the elected officials of the county. These chief executives placed the resources of their corporations and their personal efforts behind a major effort to reform local government. The public and private leaders of the county have declared Com-

[2] *Ibid.*
[3] Judith Berger, "Getting Together with Business." *Western City*, September 1979, p. 34.

PAC a success and from it several lessons about public/private partnerships have been learned. These include:

1. An explicit request must be made by the elected public officials for assistance by the business community.

2. A corporate commitment must be made for personal involvement of the chief executive officer of each participating business. This must include the availability of key corporate personnel for project work assignments.

3. A broad cross section of support for the program must be secured from major corporations and private foundations.

4. A public/private mutual embargo on publicity must be agreed upon at the outset.

5. Implementation of results through practical and deliverable products should be emphasized.

6. Attention must be given to ways of assuring avoidance of conflicts of interest and wrongdoing in the program.

7. High-quality management of individual projects must be provided.

8. Loaned executives must be provided timely and adequate orientation, and support must be provided to assure quality control of products.

9. The program must concern itself with the use of resources of related civic agencies, where possible.

10. Emphasis should be placed on monitoring the results of implementation, assuring adequate progress reporting, and completing a full project evaluation.

After several ComPAC task forces were formed, each developed a mission statement and work plan, subject to review and approval by top private and public officials involved in the program. Problems dealt with by the task forces included purchasing, cash management, personnel, computer services, management information/program budgeting, construction management, records management, business/industrial development services, and financial management.[4]

---

[4] John B. Olsen, "Applying Business Management Skills to Local Governmental Operations." *Public Administration Review,* May/June 1979, pp. 282–289.

The Allegheny County example is a comprehensive model that could easily be followed by other jurisdictions during the 1980s. Several other examples of voluntary public/private co-operation are worth mentioning:

• Cincinnati, Ohio, formed the Cincinnati Business Committee (CBC) in 1977. This committee is made up of 15 to 20 of the chief executive officers of the city's major corporations. Two key early decisions that the committee reached were that none of the chief executives could name a surrogate to act for him in CBC affairs or attend CBC meetings, and the number of projects to be conducted by the CBC was to be limited to only those in which it could make a contribution toward improvement. Projects undertaken by the CBC included city finances and organization; school financing; area development and re-development; and a series of ad hoc projects, such as energy audits and energy conservation plans.[5]

• Atlanta, Georgia, through its Chamber of Commerce, has had a Loaned Executive Program for several years. The program is triggered by a request to the Chamber from the Mayor for assistance on a specific project. The Chamber then assembles a task force to assist in the effort. Recent efforts have included advice on ways to reduce $4 million in proposed expenditures from the annual operating budget and top-level professional advice on criteria for selecting division chiefs in the fire department.

Boosterism

Earlier in this century, strong business-town relationships existed in many cities across the country. Private sector executives such as Andrew Carnegie and John D. Rockefeller established a pattern of corporate giving to communities that enhanced the character and appearance of cities where they lived and worked. This came to be known as "corporate boosterism."

After World War II, corporate boosterism waned as many corporations became preoccupied with diversification and ex-

---

[5] Charles Mechem, "Business and Government: Now Is the Time." *Public Management,* January 1979, p. 6.

pansion of their markets and as the federal government began to provide much of the urban renewal and community project funding that the private sector had provided in the past. The result was that the inner cores of cities began to decay at accelerating rates. This resulted in a loss of tax base, a decrease in population, a deterioration in city services, and an increase in crime and poverty. By the decade of the 1970s, many major companies found it difficult to persuade people to come to work for them in such cities as Detroit, Cleveland, Philadelphia, and New York. Some private firms solved their problems by relocating to the suburbs or the Sun Belt. An example of the suburbanization trend is Fairfield County, Connecticut, which now has more Fortune 500 corporate headquarters than any other county in the country. Most of the corporations that have relocated there once were in New York City.

The other solution adopted by some private firms is to stay and help their city. Notable among this group are General Motors and Ford in Detroit, Owens-Illinois in Toledo, Hallmark in Kansas City, and Johnson & Johnson in New Brunswick, New Jersey. Several private firms in Cleveland, such as Eaton Corporation, Stouffers, and Progressive Corporation, have adopted this strategy.

Progressive Corporation in Cleveland has taken a unique approach to boosterism. Because of the difficulties in recruiting top graduates from universities to come to work there, the firm is trying an experiment. During the summer months, nine interns from graduate business schools are being treated to many of the amenities of Cleveland. These include baseball games, a tour of the art museum, a trip up the Cuyahoga River, trips into ethnic neighborhoods, and open-air concerts. The purpose of these extracurricular activities is to try to convince the students that they might want to live and work in Cleveland.

The recent increase in boosterism goes well beyond private firms donating money or shrubbery. Many corporations are plunging headlong into major capital improvement projects, such as Ford Motor Company's plans to add two new office towers to the $350 million Renaissance Center in downtown

Detroit. The next section of this chapter will explore pub-lic/private partnerships in economic development in more de-tail.[6]

PUBLIC/PRIVATE JOINT VENTURES

Most public/private joint business ventures seek to address economic development problems, but the opportunity exists for joint business activities in other areas of mutual interest as well. This section discusses a number of such public/private joint ventures.

During the 1950s and 1960s, urban renewal, land clearance, and highway construction were the local government economic development watchwords. During the late 1960s and early 1970s, the emphasis shifted to the large-scale social legislation and resulting programs of the "Great Society" era. More recently, the focus has been on inner-city economic and job development, with shrinking public dollars being used to leverage private investment.

During the 1980s, a large portion of the public/private partnership efforts will be built around the revitalization of downtown America. Many new and innovative approaches to public/private joint ventures will be explored, including downtown mixed-use construction projects that include offices, hotels, retail stores, and public plazas. On the positive side, such developments can mean new jobs, including those for less-well-trained city dwellers. On the negative side, developers, anxious to maximize profits and minimize risks, will demand excessive tax abatements that may force many city taxpayers, the poor among them, to pay the way for wealthy corporations.

There is another risk; that is the proliferation of mega-structures in downtowns. These faceless, forbidding buildings may destroy the inner city's unique texture, culture, and tradition. A possible remedy is to develop good modern designs that create inviting ground-level settings.

[6] Margaret Yao, "Return to Boosterism: More Firms Seek to Improve Their Cities Instead of Giving Up and Moving Away." *The Wall Street Journal,* July 11, 1979.

Another possibility is the preservation and rehabilitation of older buildings in the central city. Several cities, such as Seattle, Boston, Hartford, Richmond, San Francisco, San Antonio, Pittsburgh, Baltimore, Milwaukee, and Denver, followed this approach during the 1970s. Their success has been remarkable. Seattle is looked to by many as the leading economic development model of the 1970s.[7]

Other examples of public/private joint ventures in economic development reveal a diversity of projects.

In Cincinnati, Taft Broadcasting Company has recently built a new headquarters building. The company has worked with the city of Cincinnati to develop a joint plan that includes tax increment financing. Taft is applying the nonschool portion of its tax dollars to the upgrading of the economically depressed neighborhood surrounding its new building. In addition, Taft is establishing an annual contribution for a neighborhood endowment fund. Each year, Taft and other businesses will contribute to the fund to assist in further upgrading the neighborhood. The fund will not be huge, but it will be substantial enough to provide seed money to assist in improving streets, lighting, and parks and to offer some low-interest loans for home improvements in the area.[8]

An increasing number of banking institutions have sought to make mortgage funds available in low- and middle-income neighborhoods. In Charlotte, the North Carolina National Bank has created a nonprofit community development corporation as a wholly owned subsidiary. Its purpose is to attract middle-class persons to purchase redeveloped housing in a district of the city that was previously run-down. The corporation then uses the profits to finance housing for lower-income persons in the same neighborhood.[9]

The Philadelphia Economic Development Corporation is one of several national models for Public/Private Economic

[7] Neal R. Peirce, "Public-Private Partnership Flourishes in Seattle." *Public Administration Times,* December 15, 1979.

[8] Mechem, *loc. cit.*

[9] Peirce, *loc. cit.*

Development Corporations (EDCs). The Philadelphia EDCs board of directors is comprised equally of business and government leaders. It receives income from its programs. It also receives funding from the city of Philadelphia, the Philadelphia Chamber of Commerce, and the state of Pennsylvania. It offers assistance in client relations, land development, and financing services to businesses locating in Philadelphia.[10]

In 1978, the life and health insurance industry initiated a new national urban initiative called "Neighborhood Response." The purpose of this new program is to help insurance companies expand their urban commitments by offering technical assistance and information to companies contemplating programs intended to help stabilize or revitalize neighborhoods. The program is being coordinated by the Clearinghouse on Corporate Social Responsibility and the Academy for Contemporary Problems in Columbus, Ohio, and Washington, D.C.

In Baltimore, Maryland, an innovative "new town" housing project has been developed. Supporters of the project, which is called "Coldspring," say it will prop up Baltimore's sagging tax base, give residents a break on housing costs, and add new vitality to the renaissance of the city. The project, which is only four miles from Baltimore's City Hall, is another approach to the effort to revitalize older, decaying downtown areas. It is a public/private partnership that provides newly constructed houses for sale to residents. Private contractors build the homes with the aid of federal dollars for sewers, streets, and other community necessities. The city has floated municipal revenue bonds to form a pool of low-cost mortgage money, which puts the cost of homes within the range of first-time buyers. The general idea is that once the project is completed (in the mid-1980s), the middle-class residents will generate enough tax revenue that one of the city's major problems—an unusually high tax rate—can be alleviated.[11]

[10] Berger, *op. cit.*, pp. 39 and 40.
[11] Deborah A. Randolph, "In-Town New Town: Baltimore's 'Coldspring' Housing Project Tests the Viability of Inner-City Revivals." *The Wall Street Journal*, October 4, 1979.

Worcester, Massachusetts, offers direct assistance to small business owners through its Worcester Cooperation Council, Inc. (WCCI). WCCI was formed in 1971 as a quasipublic, nonprofit corporation. Its focus is on giving technical advice to small business entrepreneurs in low-income neighborhoods. Its board of directors consists of 31 people, 16 of whom are appointed by the City Manager. The remainder are appointed by other organizations, such as the Chamber of Commerce. Most members represent the executive level of the private or public sector. WCCI offers three types of activities: technical assistance, equity capital to new enterprises established by low-income or minority neighborhood residents, and assistance in staffing the local development company, which assists entrepreneurs to obtain a loan from, or with the guarantee of, the U.S. Small Business Administration.[12]

In Minneapolis, a public/private partnership between the city and private developers is providing 1,700 units of new housing, a hotel, and office, retail, and restaurant facilities on the edge of downtown Minneapolis. A small city staff assigned to the development district acts as a "one-stop" point of contact for private developers wishing to participate in this tax-increment-financed redevelopment project. The staff is able to tap other resources of the city and private consultants. It solicits interest from private developers and serves as a liaison between them and the city. The staff also maintains a relationship with area community and downtown business groups. Throughout the process, a developer enjoys the consistency and convenience of working with one small group during the entire development process.[13]

Local government officials in California are initiating Economic Development Corporations on the basis of successes achieved in other cities such as Philadelphia, Dayton, and De-

[12] "Municipal Innovations 29: Strategies for Economic Development." *Management Information Service,* International City Management Association, Spring 1979.
[13] Louis DeMars, "Council Active in Guiding CBD Project." City Economic Development, *Nation's Cities Weekly,* National League of Cities, March 12, 1979.

troit. They have also learned from their own mistakes. The city of Oakland, for example, came under attack when it failed to include community leaders in its planning for an Economic Development Corporation. The process was repeated and as a result planned for two groups. The Oakland business community will spearhead the redevelopment of downtown, while neighborhood-oriented Local Development Corporations (LDCs) will sponsor and coordinate improvements in the neighborhoods. The city's Office of Economic and Community Development will funnel federal and local funds into both the EDC and the LDCs. The office will also assist them in cutting red tape in order to pave the way for investment.[14]

Public/private joint ventures for economic development have not been limited to the United States. Europe, for instance, has had some notable success stories. In Bristol, England, the waterfront area is being redeveloped and attractively landscaped for public access. The city of Bristol doesn't wait until an area is run-down before it takes action. City officials try to spot decline, either residential or commercial, and take immediate action to stem it. The city government of Bristol sees its role as active, not passive. It moves to acquire property that is derelict and prepares development plans for it. Competitive proposals are then accepted from private developers. The city makes grants available, or, if it owns the land, makes the rent low enough to encourage development. This approach has produced privately owned shops, restaurants, and restored buildings in attractively landscaped areas. *The city sees its role as one of public entrepreneur.*[15]

Another innovative approach to assisting in downtown economic development revitalization has been that taken by Control Data Corporation, a multibillion-dollar computer and technology firm in St. Paul, Minnesota. Control Data has developed an "incubator" for small businesses in innovative technology fields in a building that it owns in St. Paul's Lowertown

[14] Berger, *loc. cit.*
[15] Joe Riley, "Looking to Europe for Solutions to American Cities' Problems." *Nation's Cities Weekly,* Fall 1979.

Redevelopment Project. The incubator is called a Business and Technology Center (BTC). Two-thirds of all new jobs created in the United States since 1960 have been in small businesses; hence, the growth and nurturing of small businesses makes sense. To lower the mortality rate of new businesses, the BTC will offer them space and an array of services that entrepreneurs often cannot obtain. The payoff is expected to be that BTCs will become modest money-makers for their owners while generating needed jobs in the nation's inner cities.[16]

The Carter administration's Urban Development Action Grant (UDAG) program is another example of public dollars being used to leverage private investment for economic development. The program provides cities front-end funding in order to attract a private investor, to assemble land for a major downtown or industrial park project, or to upgrade a blighted area so as to retain an industry that provides jobs. The basic idea of UDAG is that most problems of the older American cities are economic in nature. These are high tax rates, high land costs, and a lack of jobs. UDAG was formed to address these problems. It is the first federal economic development program ever to require an "up front" private sector investment before any federal dollars flow to a project. The program is administered by the U.S. Department of Housing and Urban Development, which claims that it has leveraged almost $6 in private investment for each $1 of federal subsidy. It has been the most successful economic development program for cities during the 1970s.[17]

Basically, state and local governments use four kinds of fiscal incentives to encourage businesses to locate in their jurisdictions:

1. Creation of an attractive "tax climate."
2. Tax incentives, such as exemptions, abatements, or low-rate assessments.

[16] Neal R. Peirce, "Fledgling Urban Firms Get Incubator Care." *Jacksonville Journal,* July 23, 1979.
[17] Neal R. Peirce, "Abuses Hinder Urban Grant Program." *Public Administration Times,* September 1, 1979.

3. Provision of industrial development bonds to allow businesses to borrow at reduced rates.
4. Provision of public services, such as roads or utility hookups, at reduced costs or at no cost.

Another incentive that may catch on during the 1980s is the "enterprise zone." The idea is to halt the spread of urban decay by turning the most depressed areas of cities into enterprise zones. These would be economic areas where virtually all zoning and other governmental controls would be removed or significantly reduced. Property and business taxes would also be substantially abated. The idea would be to make the zones attractive to small business, which in turn would create jobs and return the zones to areas of economic viability.

Public/private partnerships in economic development, such as those described here, are beginning to revive many sections of America's older cities. The population drain is halting as cultural facilities, less expensive housing, and the energy crisis pull the middle class back into the cities. As long as the federal government provides a funding impetus, this trend should continue during the eighties.

Outside of the area of economic development, public/private joint ventures have not been as widely explored. However, the opportunity exists in almost any area where a mutuality of interest can be generated. A unique partnership that has been tried in some local governments is called "City Hall Neighborhoods." Under this approach, homeowners may hold down their taxes by cleaning the sidewalk and street in front of their homes. Contracts can be entered into with neighborhood organizations to provide local services in their neighborhood at low costs to local governments. Recreation programs may become almost totally staffed by volunteers. It has been predicted that by the end of the 1980s neighborhoods may become extensive service providers, even in difficult service areas such as social services.[18]

Other public/private partnerships will undoubtedly be

[18] Peirce, "Public/Private Partnership Flourishes in Seattle," *loc. cit.*

explored during the eighties. Such joint ventures might include:

A private firm managing and operating local government computer or word processing centers at reduced cost with the understanding that it can use the centers for its own for-profit work during evenings and weekends.

Sharing of vehicle maintenance facilities and equipment with a local electric, gas, or telephone utility.

Joint purchasing arrangements with a large local private firm.

Keys to fostering public/private partnerships are mutuality of trust, a clear understanding and agreement on both sides, openness, and honesty. With these elements, public/private partnerships should flourish during the decade ahead.

PRIVATIZATION

Almost every service that a local government performs could conceivably be contracted out to a private firm. Some service areas are more fraught with politics than others, making attempts to contract these out almost certain "political suicide." For example, because of traditional public perceptions and police arrest powers, police functions have generally not been contracted out.

Traditionally, local governments have contracted for a variety of services, including major construction, equipment purchases and leases, operation of a cafeteria or snack bar, vending machines, printing, auditing, compensation and benefits administration, and insurance.

In recent years, more local governments have experimented with contracting out other services and functions. Some have had great success and have saved money. Others have not. Possible contract functions include such services as grantsmanship, solid waste collection and disposal, engineering, fire, data processing, planning, buildings maintenance, and equipment maintenance.

Others are custodial, traffic engineering, transportation,

consulting and research, building and public works inspections, real estate, and legal services.

In general, the basic objective is to provide the same or better service in a more cost-effective manner.

During the eighties, the privatization of public services is expected to reach a new dimension. New approaches will be tried, and by the end of the decade it is projected that at least 25 percent of all local government services will be provided by the private sector. New private service firms will spring up and will offer a variety of services to local government under contract. These will include the following:

Circuit-riding city managers for smaller jurisdictions.
City managers and department heads.
Consulting/research.
Compensation and benefits administration.
Operation of functional departments.
Word processing/data processing/printing/copying.
Risk management.
Virtually any and all services that a city or county desires.

Leasing of equipment, such as fire trucks, computers, school buses, and garbage trucks, will also increase during the eighties. Leasing is an attractive alternative to floating bond issues. Municipal leasing is currently increasing at a rate of 15 to 20 percent per year.

A key ingredient to successful privatization efforts is a clear and comprehensive contract with a reliable firm.

12

INTERGOVERNMENTAL RELATIONS

LOCAL GOVERNMENT ADMINISTRATORS should recognize that they are now in an intergovernmental era, which David Walker of the Advisory Commission on Intergovernmental Relations (ACIR) has termed the "new fiscal federalism." The new fiscal federalism is characterized by an increasing complexity and interdependence in federal, local, and state government relationships. The traditional notion of three distinct layers of government with separate functions no longer holds up.

Scholarly writing on federalism in the last ten years progressed from description of the system as a "layer cake" (there are two or three distinct levels/layers of government) to that of a "marble cake" (intergovernmental relationships have led to a blurring of the three levels). ACIR research to date indicates both of these characterizations are now obsolete.

> . . . trends combine to suggest that a new 'supermarbleized' system (non-system would be a more appropriate term) of multiplying intergovernmental relationships has emerged. Never have the funding, functioning, administration, and personnel of so wide a range of state and especially local services been as interrelated as they are today.[1]

Some of the trends during the past two decades that have led to this complex intergovernmental atmosphere include:

[1] David Walker, "Localities and Federal Aid Under the Intergovernmental System." *National Civic Review,* January 1979.

1. Growth in government and expansion of government into roles and activities previously the province of the private sector.
2. Enormous growth in the amount and pervasiveness of federal aid programs.
3. Public awareness of urban problems.
4. Strengthened, modernized state governments and more powerful state revenue systems.
5. Increased intergovernmental lobbying, for example, the National League of Cities and other "public interest" groups.
6. More regional organizations, from federal regional councils to metropolitan councils of governments.
7. Direct federal aid to local governments, often bypassing states.
8. More federal grant conditions, more administrative requirements, and more state mandates.
9. Increase in the types of aid instruments, including block grants, revenue sharing, categorical programs, and cooperative agreements.
10. Growth in alliances between local and state government administrators of federal programs, such as highways, and the federal program administrators who oversee such local and state programs. Such alliances sometimes tend to focus on justifying both their existences rather than serving local government objectives or national purposes.

Local administrators must be aware of and learn how to operate within this new web of intergovernmental relationships. For better or worse, intergovernmental relations is a function that has to be explicitly recognized and performed by local government administrators.

Cities and counties are more closely linked with the states and the federal government than ever before. This has advantages and disadvantages. Specifically, on the one hand, less of the local budget is under local control as a result of intergovernmental aid programs. On the other hand, never before have there been so many opportunities to use federal assistance to leverage innovative projects.

Local administrators should be aware of the degree to which they are depending on federal money for basic service delivery and be attuned to federal policy/program shifts that may adversely affect future operations. The uncertain future of General Revenue Sharing and the Comprehensive Employment and Training Act (CETA) programs are examples.

In light of the proliferation of federal aid, administrators may be able to find ways to use more of it in innovative, cost-reducing programs. Examples include technology utilization programs, alternative service delivery programs, integrated grant applications, or taking advantage of innovative programs such as HUD's Urban Development Action Grant program. The criteria for the UDAG awards include the amount of investment from nonfederal sources that will be committed to the project and the number of new jobs that will be created.

This chapter first discusses several important state-local intergovernmental issues and then examines various federal-local issues and strategies.

STATE-LOCAL ISSUES

State mandates

State mandates are an area of state-local government relations that will receive a great deal of attention in the 1980s. This will be a product of the tight fiscal circumstances of local governments, concern over the proportion of local budgets that are not under local control (mandated expenditures), and the trend for states to place tax limits on local governments.

Mandates can affect both revenues and expenditures. An example of a state mandate affecting revenues is the state's exemption of certain types of property from the local property tax base. Mandates on expenditures, which will be discussed in more detail later, include state standard setting for worker's compensation; standards that increase the cost of local services, such as solid waste management regulations that make local refuse disposal sites expensive to operate; state laws that force expenditures by local governments for death benefits for retired policemen and fire fighters; or mandated programs that impose costs on local governments (for example, required local environmental impact statement preparation and review).

State mandates are usually passed to ensure that objectives deemed of statewide importance are carried out at the local level. They also result when the courts or the legislature rule that there will be statewide uniformity in the provision of a service. The Advisory Commission on Intergovernmental Relations classifies mandates into five categories.[2]

1. *Rules of the game mandates.* These concern local government organization and procedures, such as holding of local elections and form of government.
2. *Spillover mandates.* These involve new programs or expansion of existing programs in intergovernmental areas such as education, welfare, and environment.
3. *Interlocal equity mandates.* These require local governments to act or refrain from acting to avoid injury to, or conflict with, neighboring jurisdictions in areas such as land use regulation, tax assessments, and environmental standards.
4. *Loss of local tax base mandates.* These result when the state removes property or other items from the local property or sales tax base.
5. *Personnel benefit mandates.* These are circumstances where the state sets salary, wage levels, working conditions, or retirement benefits.

A 1978 ACIR survey of state mandates revealed the average state has 35 out of a possible 77 identified mandates.[3] The survey also found that the southern states do the least mandating and that where local governments contribute more than 50 percent of the state/local revenue there are more mandates. The most commonly mandated functions were solid waste disposal standards, special education programs, and worker's

[2] Advisory Commission on Intergovernmental Relations, *State Mandating of Local Expenditures.* Washington, D.C., August 1978, p. 6.
[3] *Ibid.,* pp. 7–8.

compensation for local personnel (not police, fire, or education). Social services was the area with the least mandates.

In most mandates, a key issue is whether the state partially or fully reimburses local governments for carrying out mandated responsibilities. Very few states (fewer than ten) require state compensation for certain types of mandates. Mandates, therefore, are a major local-state conflict area, and one that is likely to grow in the 1980s.

ACIR has recommended a policy of "deliberate restraint" by states with regard to mandates. The elements of this policy include the following recommendations.

1. *Review and inventory existing mandates.* The legislative and executive branch, or both jointly, should catalog existing mandates of any origin (state law, executive order, administrative rule), as well as federal and court mandates. Any future mandates should go into the catalog, and costs to local governments of any new mandates should be tabulated at the end of each legislative session. In addition, there should be a review procedure to regularly weed out unnecessary mandates.

2. *Develop a specific statement of the statewide policy objective being sought through enactment of each mandate.*

3. *Seek full state reimbursements for state mandates if state-imposed tax lids constrict local revenue-raising ability.* Lid laws seek to restrain local government growth, or else they are part of a state-local package to make sure increased state financing of public programs results in reduced reliance on, or reduced growth of, local property tax collections. There is a conflict when local governments are constrained by lids and simultaneously forced to expand activities or responsibilities because of mandates. To alleviate this conflict, ACIR has recommended that states imposing tax or expenditure limit laws either reimburse local governments for all the direct costs imposed by state mandates or exempt from all state-imposed local levy or expenditure limits those local cost increases necessitated by administrative, legislative, or judicial actions of state government.

4. *Seek partial state reimbursement when mandates require new programs or enhanced service levels in highly intergovernmental or "spillover" functions such as education, health, and highways.* The actual

percentage of reimbursement should be determined by the state legislature or executive.

5. *Seek full state reimbursement for mandates affecting local employee retirement benefits.* As was pointed out in Chapter 1 of this book, underfunded, locally administered retirement systems are a major financial management problem for cities and counties now and will continue to be in the next decade. State regulation or state takeover into one statewide system are alternatives suggested by ACIR. At the minimum, state actions that increase benefit levels should be fully reimbursed.

6. To minimize state intrusion into matters of essentially local concern, *seek full state reimbursement of all state mandates involving employee compensation, hours, working conditions, and employee qualifications.* State mandating of the terms and conditions for local public employees erodes local managerial authority and encourages "end runs" to the state legislature by activist employee organizations.

7. An effective state reimbursement program requires three *procedural safeguards:* a fiscal note process; strict interpretation of state-initiated mandates; and an appeal and adjustment provision to a designated state agency for local governments whose claims to state payments are in dispute.

In making these recommendations, which are good guideposts for the 1980s, ACIR concludes:

> These recommendations underscore the belief that those who mandate new programs should share in assuming the costs that these programs impose on local governments. . . . Taken together, these recommendations create a state policy of deliberate restraint. Comprising both procedural and substantive reform of the mandating practice, they are designed to insure fiscal "fair play" by reconciling the local government interest in setting its own fiscal priorities with the right of the state to mandate local expenditures.[4]

California's Post Commission

An interesting case study in local-state relations, which illustrates what may happen in many states in the next decade, is

[4] *Ibid.,* p. 21.

that of the California Commission on Government Reform, appointed in 1978 to investigate issues raised as a result of the passage of Proposition 13. This commission was known as the Post Commission because it was chaired by Alan Post, a former state legislative analyst. The commission had 14 members, including business, civic, labor, and government leaders. Their recommendations resulted from careful consideration of studies prepared by 57 volunteer task forces, each having three to 20 members.

The commission recommended that the state equalize expenditures for public education to meet the requirements of the *Serrano* v. *Priest* State Supreme Court decision. That 1976 decision held that financing public education principally by property taxes discriminated against children living in low-income school districts. The commission recommended that the state provide most, but not all, funding for elementary and secondary schools and community colleges. It also suggested removing legislative restrictions that reduce the flexibility of local school boards to use personnel and facilities in the most efficient and effective manner.

The Post Commission recommended state assumption of the full costs of welfare, including general relief, health costs, and, to the extent feasible, the major costs of the court system. The commission recommended that local governments continue to administer welfare programs, according to state and federal policies.

The commission also recommended that the state establish a unified retirement system for state and local public employees, with a single level of benefits. It was suggested that police and fire fighters be protected with disability insurance instead of being retired at high cost at relatively early ages. Also, it was suggested that annual salary increases be based on merit, not time-in-grade.

Another commission recommendation was state takeover of some costs of operating superior, municipal, and justice courts. The state would pay for administrators and reporters, jury commissioners, court clerks, and bailiffs. Counties would still pay for public defenders, district attorneys, and probation departments.

The commission recommended that local governments' share of the state sales tax be distributed on the basis of population, not point of origin (source of collection), and that the legislature fund all mandated costs of legislative and administrative decisions that result in new or increased costs at the local level.

Finally, the commission recommended that a state-level commission be established to (1) make recommendations to the governor and legislature on intergovernmental relationships and issues; (2) review service delivery systems at all levels of government; and (3) review, test, and evaluate criteria for the allocation of functions among governmental agencies, which can be applied in developing proposals for the reorganization of state, regional, and local governments.

Other aspects of future state-local relations are revealed in a recent National Academy of Public Administration–ACIR study funded by the Department of Housing and Urban Development. The study found that 21 states have disbursed state-local revenue sharing and/or tax funds to lessen the gap between wealthy and less wealthy local governments. These programs distribute revenues by formulas based on local population.

The study found many states beginning to introduce targeting into home rehabilitation aid programs. It found that 19 states target this aid to distressed communities; 17 states have adopted targeted rehabilitation tax incentives to encourage upgrading in designated areas; and 11 states have passed anti-redlining laws to make home ownership easier in distressed areas.

Forty-eight states have authorized creation of single or multipurpose regional authorities with regionwide financing to deliver local government services. The study showed targeted revenue aid formulas and broad grants of local taxing authority to be more prevalent in the South and West than in the Northeast and Midwest.

FEDERAL-LOCAL ISSUES

Elmer Staats, former Comptroller General of the United States, has asked, "In considering the fiscal impact of federal grant policies on states and localities facing austerity, is the federal government part of the problem or part of the solution?" He answers that General Accounting Office evaluations have shown federal grants tend to add to expenditure pressures of local governments, distort local budgets and budget-cutting efforts, and often contribute to fiscal instability.[5]

Federal grants can entice local governments to spend money on programs they ordinarily would not fund. They often force communities to continue to pay for programs initially funded by the federal government that have attracted a local constituency but are no longer in vogue in Washington, so funds have dried up.

Staats points out that federal mandates, matching, and maintenance of effort requirements and formula allocations all reward increased local spending for federally favored objectives. He notes:

> For states and localities with growing budgets, grants and their costs can be absorbed without real sacrifice from other locally funded programs. For jurisdictions experiencing budget cuts, however, these policies can become an important constraint further complicating the task of managing conflict under austerity. Jurisdictions that must cut spending are faced with a cruel dilemma. They can (1) cut spending for grants and risk loss of federal money, imposing a further loss of services on troubled local economies; or (2) cut spending disproportionately in nonfederally funded services in order to avoid triggering the loss of federal funds, thus distorting local spending priorities.[6]

This can mean cutting back on traditional, all locally funded services, such as sanitation, fire, and police. This distortion of local priorities can undermine local citizen confidence

---

[5] Elmer B. Staats, "An Era of Enduring Scarcity: Challenges and Opportunities." *National Civic Review*, January 1980, pp. 13–32.
[6] *Ibid.*, pp. 18–19.

in their local government. Thus, a Catch-22 for citizen tax revolts emerges:

> One of the great ironies of the recent tax revolt may be that movements originally sparked by disaffection and alienation of government from the people may place further distance between government and the people by increasing their dependency on external funding sources and political constraints.[7]

Optimistic signs are emerging that could help local government facing revenue reduction in the eighties. There is a strong interest on the part of the Reagan administration in reforming the federal grant system to reduce its negative impacts on local and state productivity and in simplifying and consolidating federal grants. Implementation of the Federal Grant and Cooperative Agreement Act may well result in better grantee-grantor relations.

The federal government is showing interest in more local financial management. This emphasis on better accounting, reporting, and auditing will enable local administrators and citizens to have more information on relative costs of different activities, making it easier to discuss the costs of various programs and to prioritize objectives on the basis of what citizens want to spend for what services. More quantitative program evaluation and analysis needs to be conducted at the local level.

The International City Management Association's "Report to the Profession on Future Horizons" has pointed out that local administrators may need to adopt strategies that "buy back" local independence from federal programs. The committee suggests that "the strongest constraint on local government independence and the feeling of relative powerlessness of local officials comes from the intrusion of the central government into local concerns."[8] Buying back means consciously re-

---

[7] *Ibid.,* p. 19.
[8] International City Management Association, "New Worlds of Service, Report to the Profession from the ICMA Committee on Future Horizons." October 1979, p. 11.

jecting federal offers of assistance for nonessential activities, for example, demonstration programs that might eventually have to be financed by local funds once the federal money dries up. Buying back means doing more with local funds, volunteers, and local company contributions, and less with federal programs committing local governments to activities that do not meet or may thwart achievement of local priority goals.

Another intergovernmental strategy that may become accepted is the Negotiated Investment Strategy (NIS), originated at the Kettering Foundation in Dayton, Ohio.[9] The NIS tries to strike a balance between narrow-purpose categorical grants and broad-purpose block grants. The NIS is being tested with three cities, their state governments, and federal government representatives. The cities are St. Paul, Minnesota; Gary, Indiana; and Columbus, Ohio. The NIS purpose is that these governments negotiate a set of priorities to govern federal and state aid actions in those cities.

Kunde identifies the three underpinnings of the NIS approach to be (1) realization that the programmatic approach to dealing with most urban problems doesn't work well in times of revenue reduction; (2) recognition of inherent conflicts among the three levels of government so that negotiations can deal openly with them; and (3) prohibition against creation of new organizational structures. NIS is a bargaining process.

In the tests being conducted, the federal government is being represented by the Federal Regional Council (FRC). Kunde notes "the key question regarding FRC participation in the NIS is whether individual members can subordinate the interests of their specific agencies to those of the federal governments." So far, the most cooperative federal participants in the NIS test projects have been those with local/state government or private sector experience. They seem to be able to "put themselves in the other's place" rather than merely carrying out a set of federal mission objectives.

The state governments are represented by high-level state

---

[9] James E. Kunde, "Response to Fiscal Constraint: An Intergovernmental Perspective." *National Civic Review*, February 1980.

officials appointed by the governor. The participating states identified the NIS as a promising tool to help develop a coordinated state urban policy. The local governments are represented by urban officials appointed by the mayor. They are generally from physical development functional agencies.

A key factor in the NIS is the presence of a competent, neutral mediator to oversee the negotiations. It is believed that in future NIS activities this function's cost would be shared by all three levels of government. A negotiations model, developed at the Kettering Foundation, is being used in the pilot test.

If it can be tested successfully, NIS has real potential in engendering useful intergovernmental dialogs on the rationale for federal and state spending in a given area and coordination to meet the highest-priority, locally identified needs. Extending NIS to more areas could lead "to the formation of a comprehensive, national urban policy that is built from the bottom up and based on the real needs of individual communities."[10]

Local administrators in the future should seek opportunities to be part of NIS experiments and to consider how NIS could be adapted to working with neighborhoods in discussions of city spending priorities. The success of NIS will depend, to a large extent, on whether incentives for participation can be built in at the federal level and whether there are sufficient skilled mediators who can make such a process work.

It is likely that federal assistance programs will begin to be cut back in the 1980s, but their influence on state and local government activities will still be substantial. A 1979 Report of the Comptroller General of the United States to the Congress predicts intergovernmental relations will be characterized by a fundamental tension between the increasing mutual interdependence of all levels of government and the desire of each level to preserve its own autonomy and political prerogatives.[11]

Seeking solution of ever-growing, widely publicized na-

[10] *Ibid.*, p. 98.
[11] "Perspectives on Intergovernmental Policy and Fiscal Relations." Report by the Comptroller General of the United States, U.S. GAO, June 28, 1979.

tional problems, the federal government may demand more state and local implementation of programs of national concern. In the next decade, however, local and state governments may become less tractable and less susceptible to federal "carrots" or "sticks," especially when federal policy appears too costly. This assertion of local and state prerogatives will include refusal to participate in new federal grant programs; substitution of local or state funds for federal funding of some activities; discontinuation of demonstration projects when federal funds cease; and direct challenges to federal laws that establish stringent, costly, or unnecessary standards and regulations.

13

ENERGY, THE ENVIRONMENT, AND LAND USE

THE 1980s will be characterized by a continuing energy dilemma, including major conflicts between energy development and environmental protection interests. The environment as an issue in the 1980s will be of secondary importance on the national policy agency, eclipsed by energy, economic, international, and defense issues. Environmental legislation of the 1970s will continue, however, to affect local governments in terms of funding and regulation. New or high-interest environmental issues will be hazardous waste management and disposal and water quality and supply. With regard to land use, local governments will continue to experiment with innovative strategies to manage growth as well as population decline. Energy concerns will influence land use decisions more directly.

ENERGY

In the 1980s, local government energy strategies should be concentrated in three areas:

1. Community energy management, including emergency management.
2. Use of nontraditional energy resources.
3. Resource recovery.

Local governments in the 1980s will be forced to evaluate services in terms of energy consumption. Energy conservation cannot produce great savings in some basic services; riding four police officers per car won't meet public safety objectives, just as cutting down on ambulance trips to save fuel isn't viable if emergency medical transportation is to be adequate. New public buildings must be more energy-efficient and the location of public facilities must be scrutinized more carefully. Fuel costs will prompt managers to seek optimal routing of road maintenance vehicles and productivity increases in road maintenance.

Community energy management

Communities must develop energy management plans that address the needs of their residences, industries, and commercial and institutional facilities. Federal and state agencies should provide financial and technical assistance, but the community level is where the key decision making, planning, and compromising should take place.

Communitywide energy management programs are built on the concept that the production and distribution of energy within a city or community constitute one system. Community energy management begins with an audit of community energy consumption, by source. The resulting data base can be used to project future energy demands and to set energy use reduction objectives. These audits usually combine user sampling techniques, sector-by-sector analysis, and secondary data that can be obtained from files kept by the U.S. Department of Energy (DOE).

Community energy management programs should have policy advisory committees that bring together technical experts in the community with community leaders and policy makers. Such policy advisory committees might include representatives from local utilities, consumer and environmental groups, business, and government.

The ultimate objective of community energy management programs is to devise a plan for making the community more energy-efficient. The plan should be based on accurate knowledge of energy supply, energy consumption patterns and needs, reasonable trade-offs among different sectors, and opinions of various members and leaders of the community.

Strategies that are involved in communitywide energy management planning include hiring a local government energy coordinator, developing a communitywide energy policy, and preparing a residential energy code, public education programs, and plans for integrated energy systems and resource recovery.

The city of Dayton, Ohio, has a community energy management program, funded by DOE, that appears to be a good model. It has three key elements. All the program's technical work is carried out at the University of Dayton. City staff develop recommendations and coordinate the overall effort. A policy steering committee, chaired by a city commissioner, includes citizens and representatives of industry, utilities, and the university.

The University of Dayton conducted a random sample survey of more than 2,500 residences and 1,500 commercial establishments in the city to determine consumption patterns. All the information was entered into a computer that will store, collate, and present the data as needed in the development of the city's community energy management plan.

Use of nontraditional energy sources

Community energy plans should take into account conventional energy resources such as coal and oil but should also include consideration of energy resources natural to the community, such as wood energy, solar and wind energy, or biomass conversion, such as alcohol fuel and fuels derived from wastes (industrial, agricultural, or sewage wastes). Communities should examine cogeneration in which waste heat from industrial processes is used to provide heat for other buildings or processes located at the same site.

Local government leaders should be aware of the potential of solar energy to meet part of their community's energy needs in the future. The Solar Energy Research Institute has predicted that solar cells will become economically competitive with conventional peak-load power plants by the mid-1980s.

More homes will have solar collectors for heat and photovoltaic (solar) cells for electricity. The Institute predicts that the cost of solar cells, currently about $7 per peak watt, may decrease to as little as 70 cents per peak watt by the end of the decade, making their use economically feasible for homes, businesses, schools, and factories.

Solar heating for a building costs about twice as much as a conventional system. Solar heating and air conditioning cost approximately three times as much. Payback time depends on a building's latitude, local weather conditons, and the costs of alternative energy sources. The city of Santa Clara, California, has constructed a 27,000-square-foot community recreation center that is heated and air-conditioned by solar energy. The solar system supplies about 80 percent of the building's requirements, and natural gas provides the remainder. It is expected that the higher installation costs of this system will be recouped over the life of the building as other energy sources continue to increase rapidly in price.

Communities in the 1980s may face a problem of *solar access*. This means preserving access to sunlight for buildings equipped with solar systems. Major investments in solar collection systems can be jeopardized if new buildings are constructed that block access to the sun. Within the last five years, at least nine states have passed laws allowing for the purchase of easements for light on adjacent property. The seller of the easement cannot take any action that would block sunlight from reaching the property of the easement.

Local governments in the 1980s may want to review their land use ordinances and building codes to determine whether and how their provisions affect the installation of solar systems in residential and commercial buildings. Comprehensive plans could be revised to include solar energy access components.

In New England, there has been a recent resurgence of interest in renewable energy resources. A University of New Hampshire study has concluded that "wood, low-head hydropower, solid waste, wind, thermal, solar, and conservation—all renewable resources—are the energy resources indigenous to

New England that offer the greatest hope for lower energy prices."[1]

To increase the use of wood energy, New Hampshire has increased the number of permits for do-it-yourself woodcutters and has hired contractors to cut wood to state specifications and haul it to roadsides to be sold at cost. A state law allows cities and towns in New Hampshire to give property tax credits to those who purchase wood heaters.

In 1977, in Burlington, Vermont, the Electric Department retrofitted its coal-burning generating station to burn wood chips. As a result, electricity is being produced at a cost that is one-third less than that of burning coal, the next cheapest alternative.[2]

Resource recovery

Administrators in the 1980s in many areas will be called upon to evaluate the costs and benefits of participating in or developing resource recovery facilities. Some cities will have such facilities built within their jurisdictions.

Using solid waste as an energy source will receive attention throughout the 1980s. Landfill sites are becoming scarce, and some of those that exist have developed leaching problems. Converting solid waste to energy has received federal government attention and will continue to do so. A variety of resource recovery experiments was begun in the 1970s. The results of these will help other communities in the 1980s as they contemplate developing facilities to produce energy from wastes.

The barriers to such projects usually include high risk because the technologies are new and not widely known; difficulties in finding a market for products; complexity of financing; the difficulty of coordinating studies, planning and design,

[1] George K. Lagassa, "Administering Alternative Energy Systems in a Cold Climate: The Case of New England." Paper prepared for delivery at the Annual Conference of the American Society for Public Administration, April 14–16, 1980, p. 4.
[2] *Ibid.*, p. 8.

contract arrangements, and implementation; waste aggrega-
tion and control problems; and citizen resistance to the location
of new resource recovery facilities.

Examples of the kinds of resource recovery options a community might consider include:

Generating electricity from solid waste and sewage sludge.
Recovering methane from sanitary landfills to be used as
an energy source by local businesses.
Using refuse-derived fuel to heat municipal buildings.
Using pyrolysis to produce gas suitable for industrial use.

Hempstead, New York, a small town on Long Island,
opened a resource recovery plant in which the town's garbage
is burned to produce electricity that is bought by the county
utility, the Long Island Lighting Company. In addition to
finding a definite buyer at the outset, Hempstead avoided
complex intergovernmental negotiations because it had a
ready-made site, county-owned land in an industrial-zoned
area. The town arranged with a private company, Parsons &
Whittemore, to build and operate the facility. The agreement
with Parsons & Whittemore returns 25 percent of the earnings
on the sales of recycled materials, such as ferrous metals, to the
town. Forty percent of the electricity revenues are returned to
the town. In exchange for not having to put up any capital, the
town entered into a 20-year contract with the firm.

Another example of a successful privately financed and
operated resource recovery system is the Refuse Energy Systems Company (RESCO) project in Saugus, Massachusetts. It
serves 500,000 residents in 11 towns, which have contracted
with RESCO for waste disposal for 20 years. The plant accepts
up to 1,500 tons of rubbish per day. The steam produced is sold
to a General Electric Company plant in nearby Lynn, Massachusetts. In 1976, the G.E. plant saved 311,000 barrels of oil,
and the city of Saugus received $1 million in property tax reve-
nues from RESCO. A participating town, Malden, Massachusetts, saved $36,000 in waste disposal costs.[3]

[3] *Ibid.,* p. 17.

An example of a publicly financed regional facility is the Bridgeport, Connecticut, Resource Recovery Plant, financed by the state's Resource Recovery Authority, which was established in 1973. Connecticut's plant converts garbage into a refuse-derived fuel that is sold to the United Illuminating Company, which burns it with oil to produce electricity. This facility is so successful that the Connecticut Resource Recovery Authority is studying the construction of additional plants in New Haven and at other sites.

Resource recovery efforts should begin to show more economic payoffs in the 1980s. Probably the most successful efforts will be undertaken without state and federal financial assistance and related red tape. These privately financed models may be the most profitable resource recovery ventures in the 1980s. The environmental benefits are many and, as the technologies are improved and more markets uncovered, the economic benefit of resource recovery strategies to communities will increase substantially.

ENVIRONMENT

The first Earth Day—April 22, 1970—launched the environmental movement of the 1970s, a movement that made major gains in increasing public awareness of environmental protection issues and also spawned major national legislation with tremendous impact on local governments. A brief list of some of these laws follows.

National Environmental Policy Act (NEPA). The National Environmental Policy Act was signed into law January 1, 1970; it made protection of the environment a national policy priority. Specifically, NEPA required assessments of the environmental impacts of any major federal actions. It established the environmental impact statement and a related review process that gave citizens and environmental interest groups significant new opportunities to review and comment on federal decision making. NEPA was the model for some state legislation, for example, the California Environmental Quality Act, which required environmental impact assessments for proposed state actions, as well as proposed actions at the local government level. In the early 1970s, some California counties had to impose moratoriums on building permits until they could develop a staff capacity to process environmental assessments and reviews required under the new law.

Clean Air Act Amendments of 1970. The Clean Air Act Amendments established air quality standards to be enforced by the federal government and secondary standards to be enforced by states. States were required to prepare air quality plans for federal approval. This Act was again amended in 1977 to revise compliance schedules for states and for reduction of automobile pollutants.

Federal Water Pollution Control Act of 1972 (FWPCA). This Act established a national goal for "fishable, swimmable waters" across the nation by 1983. It established the framework and funding for construction at the local level of wastewater treatment plants. This program has become the largest federally funded public works program in American history. In 1977, FWPCA became the Clean Water Act and was amended to allow more time for compliance and to authorize more funds for treatment plants.

Coastal Zone Management Act of 1972 (CZMA). The Coastal Zone Management Act provided funds for state land use planning in coastal areas. States could receive federal funds under this Act to develop coastal plans and, when these were accepted, additional funds for implementation plans. Local government consultation is required if a plan is to receive approval. Some states have gone as far as the implementation stage; others are still planning; and still others have elected to do little since this is a voluntary program.

Safe Drinking Water Act of 1974. The Safe Drinking Water Act set standards to protect public and private water supplies from health hazards. States are assigned the principal responsibility for monitoring drinking water systems.

Energy Policy and Conservation Act of 1975 (EPCA). This Act established automobile fuel-efficiency standards and industrial energy conservation goals.

Energy Conservation and Production Act of 1975 (ECPA). This

Act established an energy conservation assistance program for low-income homeowners and loan guarantees for conservation improvements, and ordered the development of thermal-efficiency standards for buildings.

Resource Conservation and Recovery Act of 1976 (RCRA). The RCRA mandated government regulation of hazardous waste from its point of generation to its final disposal in approved facilities. It also called for increased attention to resource recovery methods and sought the closing of dumps and landfills, whenever possible, at the local government level.

Comprehensive Environmental Response, Compensation and Liability Act of 1980. This law, commonly known as the Superfund, provides money to clean up uncontrolled hazardous waste sites. Local governments report sites to states, which prepare priority lists. The state pays 10 percent of clean-up costs.

In the 1980s, the trend in environmental programs will be continued federal funding, but with more state implementation. This will be true in energy, solid waste management, hazardous waste management, air and water quality, and safe drinking water. Local governments would be well advised to become involved early and frequently with these state agencies and to build strong decision-making partnerships.

Air

As the 1980s begin, most states are on the verge of having their state air quality implementation plans approved. These plans must show that minimum health standards for industrial pollutants will be met by 1982 and that minimum health standards for auto-related pollutants will be met by 1987. The plans require that cities seeking increased economic development must take additional measures to decrease pollution. The intent is to achieve more reductions in existing pollutant sources than proposed new industrial sources would generate; the resultant emissions offsets would permit new industry.

Local governments must also show how clean air will be maintained. There are three classes of clean air areas. Class I areas are allowed the smallest amount of new pollution, and Class III are allowed the highest amount of new pollution. An area can be reclassified if the state's governor and a majority of affected local governments are in agreement.

City and county economic development plans must be coordinated with state air quality implementation plans. Local governments should inventory industrial pollution sources within their boundaries to produce a useful data base. Local governments then should begin talking with local industry officials concerning compliance with state plan requirements to determine if some companies can achieve sufficient reduction (emissions offsets) so that new growth can be permitted. Local governments may find it useful to include creation of emissions offsets as a factor in development review processes. They can also encourage companies with similar emissions control problems and technical assistance or financing needs to seek joint solutions. Some local governments may want to consider setting up loan funds for industrial air pollution controls or using tax incentives to encourage emissions offsets.

Cities can create offsets in city-owned or city-regulated sources and allocate them to promote new industrial growth. Local governments should find it advantageous to seek regional cooperation in decisions about plant locations. Local zoning can be used to carry out decisions made regionally as to which areas will grow the most and will need emissons offsets.

Municipal offset rules must be written into state air quality implementation plans on the basis of state enabling legislation. Local offset rules are optional in state plans; the Act requires only local government consultation. It is likely, however, that states will welcome offset plans and policies designed at the local government level in conjunction with industry, to permit maximum growth with acceptable air quality levels.

Water

The year 1983 is the deadline set by the Clean Water Act of 1977 (amending the FWPCA of 1972) for providing secondary treatment for local governments unable to proceed with wastewater treatment plant construction through circumstances beyond their control. The foremost problem has been delays in obtaining federal funds. Another problem has been the initial federal encouragement of high-technology and expensive wastewater treatment plants that really didn't meet the needs of smaller communities. In the 1980s, federal and local emphasis will be on more cost-effective and appropriate technological solutions to wastewater treatment. The Clean Water Act built in financial incentives for innovative rather than conventional treatment methods.

An example of an innovative, small community alternative is the Hercules, California, wastewater treatment facility. Hercules is a community of 7,000 that expects its population may triple in this decade because of its location 30 miles north of San Francisco. The community decided to build an innovative, self-contained facility rather than tie in with larger systems. The Hercules facility has raw sewage enter earthen ponds where 30 to 50 percent of the solids settle and are anaerobically converted to methane gas. This gas is piped to a generator to produce power for the plant. The sewage then goes to a solar-heated, greenhouse-covered lagoon. The water hyacinths in the lagoon absorb sewage and toxic chemicals. These hyacinth plants can be harvested to produce methane gas. The wastewater goes to additional lagoons to feed more plants or can be processed into fertilizer or animal food. After advanced treatment and filtration, fresh water is discharged for use in irrigation or groundwater recharge. Hercules and the small firm that built the plant estimate this process costs less than half of the construction and operating costs of conventional, high-technology plants.

Other sewage treatment needs in the 1980s will be to find economic and environmentally sound ways to dispose of sludge, to integrate the operations of solid waste disposal systems and sewage treatment facilities, and to monitor and repair sewer system infrastructures.

Some cities and counties in the 1980s will incur costs as a result of the Safe Drinking Water Act, which does not provide financial assistance for its implementation. Communities that operate water systems should examine their water rates to be sure they cover the real costs of providing safe drinking water. These costs include developing a good source of water, treating and distributing it, establishing a good monitoring system, and providing trained personnel to operate the facilities.

As was discussed in Chapter 1, problems with water supply will begin to be recognized in the 1980s. The importance of urban water supply issues and the need to conserve water through pricing will be well recognized by the end of this decade.

Hazardous wastes

In early 1980, the Environmental Protection Agency issued a final set of regulations to control the more than 40 million tons of hazardous wastes produced in this country each year. All companies that produce, transport, or dispose of hazardous wastes were required to notify EPA of their activities by August 1980, in order to continue their operations. The regulations identify which wastes EPA considers hazardous, define broad requirements for hazardous waste storage and disposal facilities, and set standards for state hazardous waste management programs.

The regulations term a waste hazardous if it is toxic, ignitable, corrosive, or reactive. The regulations list more than 80 industrial process wastes and more than 400 hazardous chemicals and discarded commercial products. Small generators, firms that produce less than 1,000 kilograms of an identified hazardous waste per month, are exempted from the regulations. It is likely by the mid-1980s there will also be regulations issued to cover these small generators.

All firms that store, treat, or dispose of a hazardous waste are required to apply for a permit from EPA. Permit requirements include technical monitoring, regular inspections and reporting, training of personnel, and emergency plans. Noncomplying facilities will be shut down by EPA.

Local governments must be sure that the landfills they operate do not accept hazardous wastes for disposal. It is recommended that local governments take an active role in monitoring industrial compliance with EPA regulations.

In 1980, Superfund legislation was passed by Congress. The Superfund is to conduct hazardous waste investigations, begin prosecutions, and clean up sites. An estimated $300 million to $600 million annually would be generated for this purpose from taxes on petroleum and chemicals industries. Local governments should report uncontrolled hazardous waste sites to the state governments in order to be eligible for Superfund clean-up funds.

LAND USE

Traditional zoning regulations that came into use after World War II were designed to regulate the style of building and types of activities allowed in a particular area. Community land use management involved control over the type and location of development and its density and sought the construction of buildings that met certain safety and environmental standards.

Today, local government land use management is a much expanded activity involving a whole spectrum of issues. These issues range from environmental (whether new development will deplete water supplies, disrupt estuaries, or be situated in geologically unsafe areas) to social and racial issues (whether growth management objectives seek to protect middle- and upper-class residential areas from the encroachment of low-income housing) to energy issues (whether a local government should make it a policy to permit only in-fill development). Federal air and water quality legislation and new programs such as flood insurance have accelerated the increase in expanded local government concerns and responsibilities as to land use and growth management.

A major new concern of communities is whether new development will be an economic plus or an economic drain. The costs of providing municipal supporting services and facilities such as roads, sewers, and schools must be calculated and compared with revenues that will be generated by the new development.

The assumption that new development will pay its own way is being seriously questioned. With the passage of measures such as Proposition 13, which limit property taxes, and the rise in service delivery costs because of inflation, labor, and materials costs, local governments will find it increasingly necessary to devise ways to systematically measure the costs and benefits of urban growth. Cities will have to place much more emphasis on economic impacts in their development review processes. Unfortunately, as a result of Propositon 13-type efforts, communities will probably have less funds for analytical staff who can develop good cost/revenue data on which to reach sound land use decisions.

A systematic review would first analyze service delivery: What will be the initial and long-term service requirements of the development, as well as of the community surrounding the development? The second component is a cost/revenue analysis based on the service delivery profile, which provides information on the capital, operating, and maintenance costs associated with the new development. The results of both analyses should be integrated into the standard procedures for land use review, environmental and community review, and subdivision, permit, site plan, and similar requirements. Thus, the local decision makers will be provided a comprehensive set of data on the proposed new development.

Facing the prospect that new developments may have negative fiscal impacts, many local governments are now requiring developers to pay up-front "impact fees" to help meet the costs of providing public improvements to new developments. Others require developers to build parks and roads and provide lighting and maintenance. Local governments are also looking more favorably on new developments that can generate other revenues, such as commercial establishments that will generate sales tax revenues.

During the last ten years, many communities across the nation have experimented with a variety of growth management strategies. In Oregon, for example, the state sets broad standards that cities and counties must meet in their comprehensive plans and zoning ordinances. Communities establish urban growth boundaries outside of which no development is allowed for 20 years. Local plans are reviewed by the state Land Conservation and Development Commission. The state standards favor growth near existing service infrastructures and encourage communities to ascertain their long-range needs and goals.

Some communities such as Ramapo, New York; Boulder, Colorado; and Montgomery County, Maryland, have tried to limit growth through their control over the extension of government-owned public works, such as water and sewer lines. This gives local government control over the amount, location, and timing of new development. Other communities ration building permits or set quotas on the number of housing units that can be built in a particular area during a particular time frame. Still other communities base growth management programs on the desire to prevent depletion or deterioration of a valued resource such as farmland, potable water, historic features, or open space.

Many of the types of programs mentioned here will be used and refined throughout the 1980s by local governments. The legal questions, such as the taking issue, right to travel, and regional welfare, will be clarified. Some promising land use strategies for local governments in the next decade include innovative zoning and development agreements.

Innovative zoning

Innovative zoning provides a means for a community to actively encourage quality development compatible with community goals. This is in contrast to conventional zoning, which takes a negative approach and concerns itself with all the things that a developer cannot do. Three important types of innovative zoning are planned unit development, incentive zoning, and impact zoning.

Planned unit development (PUD). Planned unit development establishes a certain area where conventional zoning regulations can be more flexible, subject to a specific site plan approval. For example, a developer may be granted an increase in unit density in exchange for setting aside a certain amount of open space within the development. Commercial and retail facilities may be mixed in with housing on the proposed site.

PUD can range from simple cluster zoning to complete new town proposals such as Reston, Virginia, or Columbia, Maryland.

Average PUD site sizes are between 20 and 40 acres. The majority of these are fairly high-density residential. Generally, planned unit developments have contributed to better community design because of more flexibility and the preservation of open space and natural features. Higher densities generally allow for lower housing costs.

Incentive zoning. Incentive zoning is the process whereby a developer is granted specific public concessions, such as increased density or building height, in return for a specific contribution, such as a public beach. As incentives, a local government might offer tax relief; street improvements; subsidies; height, density, or unit size changes; or additional uses. In return, a developer might preserve historic features; develop a public park, beach, or plaza; preserve public beach access; build a library; or decrease housing costs. Exact trade-offs are usually written into community zoning ordinances.

Impact zoning. Impact zoning seeks to establish a framework for negotiation by the use of specific performance standards and evaluation methods. Approval is made contingent on the proposal having positive or neutral impacts on the community. It requires an environmental impact statement. An example of a performance standard might be 25 percent open space or no increase in traffic congestion from the site. Sophisticated impact zoning techniques include studying community carrying capacities and comparing these with proposed service, fiscal, and environmental impacts that would occur if the proposed development were built.

Making use of impact zoning requires a strong data base and trained analytical staff working for the local government. Local governments should select what types of zoning they will use on the basis of community goals, availability of data, and amount of in-house technical capability. In essence, the difference between conventional zoning and innovative zoning is the kind and amount of information required and the specific approval criteria required.

The steps for instituting an innovative zoning program are as follows:

1. Determine community goals and objectives through a citizens committee appointed for this purpose.
2. Direct planning staff to gather information on the community to ensure a technical data base.
3. Convene the citizens committee and staff at meetings to review and validate the data base.
4. Direct them to develop proposals for innovative zoning and describe them in a brochure or newspaper insert that is concise and understandable for citizens.
5. Arrange small neighborhood meetings to discuss the proposals.
6. Hold a formal public hearing to discuss and adopt the proposals.[4]

Development agreements

Another new tool is the development agreement, a flexible agreement made between developers and local governments that sets forth rules to govern development as it proceeds through the approval process. The League of California Cities has done pioneering work in the legalities and procedures involved in development agreements.[5]

Development agreements are not substitutes for existing land use approval requirements. They are similar to the PUD concept, except that in the development agreement both parties commit themselves to proceed in accordance with the agreement. The local government agrees that future land use decisions with regard to a particular development will be made in accord with the laws and policies in effect when the agreement was signed. This makes the future much less uncertain for the developer. In return, the developer agrees to construct cer-

---

[4] Adapted from *Innovative Zoning: A Local Official's Guidebook.* Prepared for the U.S. Department of Housing and Urban Development by Rahenkamp, Sachs, Wells and Associates, Inc., with the American Society of Planning Officials and David Stoloff, November 1977.

[5] "Development Agreements." *Western City*, March 1980, pp. 13–15.

tain improvements, provide certain public services, develop according to a certain time schedule, or make other commitments that the local government usually has no legal authority to ask the developer to perform.

Development agreements are usually for a minimum of one year up to a maximum of three years. A development agreement should be considered only for a large, multiphase development that involves substantial investments, because such agreements require time for the local government to amend ordinances. They require more paperwork and time for both parties in the initial stages, but they may ultimately have major payoffs for all concerned. Communities have more knowledge of what will happen to a particular area in the future, and developers will encounter less uncertainty in subsequent reviews by the local governments.

14

STRATEGIES FOR CHANGE IN
LOCAL GOVERNMENT

THIS BOOK offers proven ways of cutting municipal costs and increasing the efficiency of local government. It will join a growing reference library of books designed to help municipal managers deal with the problems of revenue reductions and increased productivity.

Municipal associations, professional management organizations, and federal government agencies publish pamphlets and books on government efficiency and sell subscriptions to newsletters describing the latest device or technology to cut costs. Local government managers may attend conferences, seminars, workshops, and equipment trade shows that demonstrate cost-saving ideas and efficiency-increasing techniques. All this activity and interest would indicate that most local governments excel in efficiency and inventiveness. Unfortunately, this is not so.

Most local government managers continue to do things as they always have in the belief that it may be all right for some other local government to try a new idea or device, but they could never get away with it in their city or county. Opposition from the union, the city council, the county commission, or the community may be the reasons given.

This chapter will discuss the problem of fear of innovation. All the good ideas in the world are worthless unless they are put to some use. Good intentions and conference attendance by themselves will not make the next decade one of local government renaissance. Only the application of the knowledge we now have about improving the performance of government will let local government meet the needs of its citizens within the fiscal limits the economy and the taxpayer revolt have created.

INCREASING OPPORTUNITIES FOR INNOVATION

Let us examine ways managers can increase opportunities for innovation and improve chances for success. If the line of resistance to change were in a constant place, evaluating the possibilities of success for a particular innovation or change would be much easier. But events constantly alter the position of that tolerance line, and it is in a different place for different issues and at different times. For example, there may be a great deal of room for innovation in the fire service but little in the police service. A tight budget may increase willingness to accept innovation in highway construction but reduce it in refuse collection services. The line of resistance is not in the same position in one local government as it is in another. This means that one city's or county's experience with change is not always a useful guide in introducing that same change in another jurisdiction.

The first step for the would-be innovator is to locate the line of resistance for a particular issue and take full advantage of the opportunity for change it gives. The best method for locating the line of resistance on a particular issue is to use the trial balloon, or run-it-up-the-flagpole-and-see-who-salutes method. Fortunately, there are a number of warning signals before one reaches the line of resistance. But a manager who is convinced of the reasonableness of an idea for change may overlook the warning and cross the line of resistance without being aware of it. If relationships with the council or commission and the community have been good, that manager probably will survive the resulting storm, but the chances for success the next time he or she introduces a change will be diminished.

In addition to the well-meaning manager who blunders over the line of resistance to change, either through ignorance or in an excess of enthusiasm, some managers deliberately adopt a policy of brinkmanship. Such a manager often accomplishes a great deal and is certainly fun to watch at work. He or she is constantly at war with members of the council or commission, the news media, or some other segment of the community. The immediate results of kamikaze managers are often impressive, but the improvements they bring to government often don't last longer than their job tenure. The objective of good management should be to create an atmosphere that encourages innovation, thought, efficiency, and individual development. Knowing where the line of resistance to change is on any issue and developing the skills to increase the tolerance for change can create a management structure that increases individual innovation and resultant improvements in operating effectiveness.

This chapter will deal with three issues: locating the resistance to the change line; factors external to the manager that change the position of this line; and ways in which the manager can change it by personal action.

The first requirement for locating the line of resistance to change is a thorough knowledge of the community. It is important to know the position of each council or commission member on any issue and what the newspaper's editorial policy is likely to be when the issue is raised. Informal discussions of the issue with members of the council/commission can be helpful if they are kept as general as possible. They provide an ideal opportunity to educate the council or commission member and to suggest to him or her a number of alternate courses of action. A serious mistake managers make is to expect council or commission members to instantly take a stand on an issue before they have had an opportunity to thoroughly understand it or to understand their constituents' interest in it.

The reporters who cover the city hall or the county courthouse on a day-to-day basis can help a manager discover the line of resistance to change on a given issue. They often have their own opinions which may or may not reflect the editorial opinions of their newspapers. It is worth knowing what these opinions are and how strongly they are held. Opinion polling and attitude sampling can give a manager a general feeling of the public's interest in any given issue and how strongly various opinions are held. The leadership of neighborhood organizations and other community leaders are sounding boards that can help a manager measure support or opposition on a particular issue. Not only will a manager locate the line of resistance by understanding the community but he will also learn what segments of the community have a particular interest in the issue at hand.

As the manager attempts to locate the line of resistance to change on a specific issue, one of the most frequent responses will be, "We tried that before and it didn't work." An examination of the issue will often reveal that what was tried and allegedly failed was the will of the bureaucracy and not the idea, or it was an entirely different problem and solution.

What happened in the past has great value in helping to predict the future location of the line of resistance to change. The passage of time, however, often changes the problem, the people who were concerned with it, and attitudes in general, so that what happened in the past is not a precise guide to the future.

Because the line of resistance may change during the implementation of any new program, it is sometimes difficult to predict the effect or consequences of the proposed change. One way to handle this is to take all reasonable precautions and then start implementing the change. If things get too complicated, a manager can always back off.

Another less risky method by which a manager may evaluate resistance to change for a given issue is to create a model that will let him or her predict the consequences of the change without having to make a major commitment to it. Many city or county services, such as refuse collection, police patrol, and the distribution of fire stations, lend themselves very well to the modeling technique. Even if the model isn't precise, the effort to quantify will give a manager some new insights into the proposed change and the effect it may have on the community.

Similar to the model, but a little more risky, is the pilot project. On a number of issues a manager may create a small-scale test of what he or she wants to do, one that will minimize the consequences of failure. This will also give the manager an opportunity to assess the opposition to the particular change. The difficulty with pilot projects is that they may not predict what will happen on a larger scale. They should, however, at least reveal problems of management and community acceptance that will help the manager decide whether to go on with the project.

Experience will help a manager monitor the council or commission, news media, and public as an issue develops, so that he or she can accurately assess the chances of success on any issue. It is often better to back off if defeat is inevitable, because that leaves the option of trying again when chances are better. An old and wise manager once said, "Change is to government as a racehorse is to a track. A horse will be around again if you don't shoot it the first time."

The art of perceiving changes in the position of the resistance line caused by external events lies in utilizing those influences to increase the likelihood of successful innovation. Often the changes that influence the position of the line of resistance are at first perceived as disasters. No matter how bad an event may initially seem, it almost always creates an opportunity to initiate change. A good example of chaos creating opportunities for change was the havoc wreaked on the Mississippi Gulf Coast in 1969 by Hurricane Camille. Out of that disaster came much better emergency preparations planning that helped save lives and reduce property damage when a hurricane hit much of the same area in 1979. The fiscal crisis that will be with most governments throughout the 1980s will create many opportunities to innovate in areas of productivity and efficiency.

Revenue reduction, cost increases, and taxpayer dissatisfaction all reduce the resistance to change on the part of citizens, council/commission, and employees. Natural and manmade disasters give the manager an opportunity to review how the city/county delivers a given service and to introduce changes in that delivery system.

The discovery of dishonesty on the part of public employees offers opportunities for introducing changes. If the manager is willing to look at fundamental changes in the system rather than cosmetic changes that most likely will increase costs, the discovery of corruption or inefficiency in a governmental operation is a golden opportunity for making changes that have been deferred too long.

Systems that seem to function satisfactorily, even if inefficiently, often break down and reveal their true nature under pressure. A flood, a large snowstorm, an employees' strike, and similar disasters provide the opportunity to reexamine what local government is doing and to make some substantial changes in its operation. There will also be some opportunities for change that will arise from positive actions. New federal programs will create new, if limited, fiscal resources for local governments, and local periods of prosperity will bring new or increased tax revenues. If the new revenues produced by windfalls of this sort are perceived as a signal to return to the "good old days" of expanding governmental services, however, they will only increase the problems local government will face in the future.

The prospects of increased revenues rejuvenate morbid bureaucracies and create a different set of problems for the manager than those caused by failures of public systems. The failure of a public system to function well in the face of a challenge often brings about the least useful reaction from its managers at the very time that the organization should be most free to innovate and that creativity from employees is most needed. The organization is likely to turn in upon itself, becoming more centralized, more cautious, and more vocal in defending the way it has been doing things. The result of this "wagon circling" is a large expenditure of energy, both inside the organization and in its relationships with the rest of the world. Affixing and avoiding blame become a preoccupation inside the organization and with its outside detractors and supporters. The effect of this is more likely to produce another set of regulations, checks, and controls rather than any positive changes in the organization. If anything, the organization becomes more cautious and its employees less likely to advocate any change that might attract attention to them.

The skilled manager can see beyond the point of affixing blame and realizes that the opportunity for positive change in the organization has been increased by the anxiety about inquiry into reasons for past failures. Positive approaches to fundamental management improvement will be welcomed by the organization's detractors and its defenders.

The more closely a manager examines the location of the line of resistance to change, the more he or she realizes its position is constantly changing and that this position is affected by a wide variety of events. Watching these changes for opportunities to introduce new ideas and for warnings of when to slow down will improve the efficiency of government, with a modest risk to the manager. The manager need only have a general idea of what he or she wants to accomplish and a closet full of projects to select from when the opportunity presents itself. Over a period of time, major changes can be made in the way the government operates, and the manager will find that the tolerance to change will increase as the organization performs more efficiently and as the manager anticipates problems and implements solutions.

The resulting rate of progress will probably satisfy most managers and will certainly improve the efficiency of most governmental organizations, but it may not be fast enough to suit some managers. A manager may decide he or she would like to be able to influence the line of resistance to change without having to wait for external events to accomplish this. For this manager, the ability to manipulate the level of resistance to change is of value. The deliberate and planned increase in an organization's tolerance to change can be risky, but the feeling of accomplishment and control it provides far outweighs the risks involved.

It is this ability to influence the line of resistance to change that lies at the very heart of the art of management and, like all art, it is something that has to be practiced to be learned. Some may object that this involves manipulating people and events, a proper role for the elected leader but not for the appointed manager, or that there is something inherently wrong with trying to change attitudes and circumstances to achieve a predetermined goal. Manipulation is only a more realistic description of leadership, and a proper inquiry into its morality should examine its methods and its goal, but not its use.

Following are some suggestions that the manager can use to influence the position of the line of resistance to change as it applies to a specific local government. With experience and reflection most managers will be able to add to this list.

Often the manager is the only person who is likely to accept leadership in the publicly unexciting project of increasing the efficiency of government. No end of leadership will be discovered if you talk about cutting taxes and increasing services, but that leadership will evaporate if you are interested in increasing accountability and productivity. A smart manager will not confuse leadership with public credit for accomplishment. He or she will work with the elected officials to encourage them to take public leadership in improving governmental performance and will give them credit for accomplishment. The manager's reward for increasing efficiency in government is in knowing that he or she did it and in seeing the staff stretch to exercise their creativity.

Because of the groups they represent or because of their peculiar association with an issue, some people are able to increase the level of resistance to change on some issues more than others. The shop steward in the local government garage is much more likely to get the mechanics in that garage to accept work standards than is a bright, young budget analyst from the management office. The manager who wants to increase the tolerance of change in the organization will spend time understanding who has a special interest in any planned change and what that interest is. A manager will try to develop leadership on the issue of concern from among the people who are affected by it and will even try to convince the affected group that the desired change was really their idea.

The quality of support for the change a manager wants to make is important, but so is the size of that support. Special interest groups have demonstrated the effectiveness of creating the illusion of broad support from relatively small groups. If, at the first council/commission discussion of a change the manager proposes, all the council/commission sees is a chamber full of opponents, it may be difficult to convince the elected members that they are the only people in the local government who are opposed to the proposed change. A group of supporters who appear at the start of any discussion will not only convince the council/commission that there are two sides to the issue but will produce much better balanced media coverage.

The most difficult problem to solve in an attempt to increase the level of tolerance to change is that the people who are opposed to a given idea have a much stronger motivation to oppose it than its supporters have to support it. The effect of self-serving opposition is to distort the apparent position of the line of resistance to change. Public attitude and opinion polls are helpful tools the manager can use to accurately locate the line of resistance to change and to demonstrate its location to members of the council/commission. They are also helpful in demonstrating to the media the narrow base of support that most active opposition groups have.

There are few issues that do not have current or potential partisans on both sides. The thoughtful manager will identify both and be sure the group that supports his/her ideas for change are heard from. As an example of this principle, imagine the manager who has decided the city/county could make substantial savings by privatizing a section of the refuse collection in the jurisdiction. If the first public discussion of the idea at the council/commission meeting is attended by 500 refuse collectors, organized by their union representative, discussing how these poor people are going to be thrown out of jobs, the issue suddenly becomes, both to the council/commission and the public at large, the prosperous, well-upholstered city/county manager versus the poor, hardworking garbageman. A little thought on the manager's part would have brought the realization that there probably are as many poor people who would benefit by privatization and that the private collectors could probably fill the council/commission chamber with "Ma" and "Pa" operators who are struggling to make a living with one truck. The result would have been a balanced picture of the effect of the change that would not pit the manager against the group and would, in effect, develop allies and sympathy.

Unfortunately, there are not always organized groups who will support the manager's position, and it may be necessary for the manager to organize his or her own support. Citizen volunteers who explore and recommend solutions to problems are often an effective means to develop a constituency for change. Neighborhood organizations and citizen action groups who have the opportunity to think through a problem can sometimes put the manager in the position of appearing to be pushed into recommending a change that was already intended. There is often an unspoken competition between the council/commission and the manager that groups opposed to the manager's recommendation can exploit. If the council's/commission's perception is that the manager is being pushed by an outside group, this possibility is much less likely to develop.

The level and direction of media coverage has a major influence on the location of the line of resistance to change on most issues. By choosing what issues to cover and by the extent of the coverage, the media can decrease or increase the manager's chances of success in getting a particular innovation adopted. Unfortunately, many managers confine their media contacts to news conferences and complaints to the editor about stories they didn't like. The more open the manager is in dealing with the media, and the more he or she is willing to spend time discussing ideas and plans with them, the better the coverage will be.

The use of a paid public relations person to act as a buffer between the manager and the media is a mistake. The media perceive it as an attempt to avoid them and the taxpayers see it as a use of their money to trumpet the virtues of a government they probably don't like anyway. It is wise for a manager to remember that radio and television are concerned with audio and visual images and that controversy creates better images than agreement. It is imperative that there is always an image friendly to the manager's position available to counteract the image that opposition presents.

Most reporters are anxious to present both sides of an issue. It is up to the manager to see that his or her side has as much visual appeal as that of the opponents. A group of city/county employees protesting layoffs is a less damaging public issue if it is balanced by a group of citizens demanding a tax cut.

Radio and television generally deal with ideas that can be explained in less than 30 seconds. A good manager will practice presenting ideas in a short time frame and will understand that most reporters from television and radio don't really understand what is going on in local government and don't have time to learn. Because of the nature of the print media, newspaper reporters have a great deal more time to explain issues and usually are willing to do some research to develop enough background to explain the issue well. The more time the manager can spend with newspaper reporters, the less likely a story in the paper will be superficial. Although editors and publishers do not write the day-to-day news, they generally make the decisions about what news will be featured and what the editorial position of the newspaper will be. It is therefore a good idea for the manager to report to them periodically about what's going on in local government.

The business community, in theory at least, is an ally of the manager in wanting to improve productivity and efficiency in government. The business community can contribute valuable expertise and, by its approval of a plan the manager wants to implement, can substantially raise the line of resistance to change. It can also help the local government gain a reputation for innovation and productivity that will increase receptiveness to new ideas in the future.

15

TOWARD THE YEAR 2000

THIS BOOK has attempted to identify numerous trends and conditions that will be present in the 1980s and will affect the activities of local government administrators. Certain themes, such as managing in an era of revenue reduction and improving productivity, appear in almost all chapters.

Urban strategies for the eighties have been considered from various perspectives, from functional considerations such as personnel and land use management to cross-cutting ideas and tools such as the introduction of new technologies and new organizational structures. The book emphasizes practical activities, not theory, and includes several real-life examples and case studies.

This chapter will present a cautionary note to public administrators who must develop ways to deliver services most efficiently and equitably in this new decade.

The principal message of this chapter is that as contemporary life and society increase in complexity, and as technological change becomes more rapid, it is important that public policy not lose its perception of human scale. Government programs, especially at the local level, should nurture an awareness of the need for attention to human scale. Although government administrators must know the big trends and how to deal with federal programs and with complicated, interrelated economic and environmental factors, they should not foster or encourage programs that are dehumanizing, that don't treat people as people, or that threaten to take away anchors of stability in people's lives.

Warren Bennis has suggested that in looking toward the future there is a need to develop society's institutions "on a human scale which permits the individual to retain his identity and integrity in a society increasingly characterized by massive urban, highly centralized governmental, business, educational, mass media, and other institutions."[1] Local government institutions should be responsive to, and interested in, human beings.

Local governments can foster the spirit of community by observing traditional holidays with special activities. They can sponsor celebrations and parades in honor of city or county history, ethnic neighborhoods, or local agricultural or industrial products. Community pride and participation are old-fashioned concepts that can have new currency in the coming decade.

Local governments can decentralize and streamline their procedures so that citizens aren't frustrated in their dealings with the government. They can also promote and coordinate citizen volunteer efforts such as the maintenance of common areas or the development of neighborhood crime prevention efforts. These citizen efforts can be publicized and rewarded.

Another promising idea that reinforces this theme is that of mediating structures, a concept propounded by Peter L. Berger and Richard John Neuhaus.[2] Berger and Neuhaus use the phrase *mediating structure* to mean families, neighborhoods, churches, and ethnic subgroups, which are between the individual in his or her private life and the large institutions of public life. They contend that government, in seeking to help individuals, too often designs programs that ignore mediating structures and that this is one reason government social pro-

---

[1] Warren G. Bennis, "A Funny Thing Happened on the Way to the Future." *Optimizing Human Resources.* Gordon L. Lippitt, Leslie E. This, and Robert G. Bidwell, Jr., Eds. Reading, Mass.: Addison-Wesley, 1971, p. 26.
[2] Peter L. Berger and Richard John Neuhaus, *To Empower People: The Role of Mediating Structures in Public Policy.* Washington, D.C.: American Enterprise Institute for Public Policy Research, 1977.

grams haven't been working very well. An example is the government providing funds for an elderly person's care in a government institution when, instead, it could provide payments to a neighbor or relative who otherwise could not afford to take in the elderly person. This alternative would be less disruptive for the elderly person and less costly to the government than institutionalization.

It is possible taxation policies can be altered to encourage mediating structures, such as tax exemptions for families who care for elderly dependents. Another possibility is for government to encourage more private sector activities that foster mediating structures. For example, many firms now provide services to their transferred employees, such as location of new housing or finding jobs for spouses. Companies might also be encouraged by government to provide child care or retired persons programs.

If you ask people where they would turn in time of trouble, the choice usually begins with family and then goes on to neighbors, the church, and friends. That is the basis of the mediating structures concept. Government social services programs always rank toward the end of the lists of places to which people in trouble would turn. And yet, it is these programs that receive showers of funds to help people in trouble.

Government programs should be examined to make sure they are not (often inadvertently) weakening mediating structures. In the 1980s, a rethinking of government programs might look to neighborhoods, small-scale social organizations, and churches as more active participants in social services, with some federal support, but without massive federal intrusion.

A two-tier approach to government service delivery, proposed by the Committee on Economic Development 11 years ago, still seems to make sense for the future.[3] It recognizes the importance of neighborhoods and at the same time provides for service delivery in ways that take advantage of economies of scale.

---

[3] Committee for Economic Development, *Reshaping Government in Metropolitan Areas*. New York: Committee for Economic Development, 1970.

The two-tier approach is based on a thorough analysis of functions within a given area. Some functions would be provided on a centralized, areawide basis; others would be performed by neighborhood "governments." Power would be shared between the areawide government and the neighborhoods. The appeal of this proposal is the ability to address on a wide scale problems such as pollution and physical development and, at the same time, to allow citizen participation at the neighborhood level in other governmental functions and decision making.

An indication that metropolitanization of urban and suburban functions is on the rise can be seen in the increasing role counties are taking in delivering services. Counties have taken over numerous functions of the cities within their boundaries. These include welfare and corrections and medical facilities. Other municipal services are provided by counties to cities within their boundaries under contractual arrangements. This may signal only the beginning of local reorganizations in which neighborhoods and regional government entities (counties or not) become the two principal forces in substate government.

Another aspect of the return to human scale in program design can be seen in the trends in some major federal programs. Interstate highway systems, for example, are no longer being built inexorably; considerations in decisions to build more beltways now include concern for downtown businesses and further erosion of life in central cities.

The federal sewer construction grants program was changed in 1977 to provide financial incentives for innovative and alternative methods of wastewater treatment, not just more construction of conventional, high-technology plants without regard to community needs or scale. In rural communities, appropriate technologies such as septic systems are being encouraged. Funding small-scale home energy projects and urban homesteading are other examples of federal programs in which human beings are considered as the focal point.

A switch to more block grants instead of so many specialized category grants would continue another healthy trend of recognizing community and regional differences and the need to set local priorities locally. More public policy activities are beginning to recognize that there is value in diversity and that human beings, living in different ways in different geographic areas, are the source of this rich diversity.

Some of the recent trends stem from the Carter administration's community conservation policy. This consists of a set of nonregulatory guidelines issued in 1979, pointing out that federal actions in the past have often reinforced patterns of urban sprawl. The objectives of the policy are to keep federal programs from exerting a negative influence on urban economic patterns and to prevent the government from inadvertently investing in urban conservation and urban sprawl simultaneously. The guidelines establish a review and appeals process. The chief elected official of a community may request the federal government to conduct a community impact analysis when a private development is significantly assisted by federal funds or actions, or when the local government can identify how such funding or action will damage existing commercial areas. If the analysis reveals sufficient negative impacts, the federal funds may be cut off.

Another aspect of the return to consideration of human scale that should guide public sector officials is recognition of the role of positive incentives—what really motivates people to do things. For example, if you want more federal researchers to transfer technology and research results to local governments, then there needs to be a reward system and a suitable career ladder. Agency heads must recognize the value of technology transfer if agency staff members are to have incentives to make it happen.

Finally, the biggest challenge of the next 20 years will be to rekindle hope and enthusiasm in people who are scared and depressed about the future and who have lost their faith in government.

People increasingly confront grim predictions about the future. A committee appointed by the president in 1977 to examine the state of the world on the brink of the twenty-first century issued in 1980 the Global 2000 Report.[4] That report predicts a world in the year 2000 that is more crowded, more polluted, less ecologically stable, and more subject to disruption than the world today. Specters of shortages abound. Energy and water are two such; others are loss of agricultural resources and shortages of domestically produced critical materials, such as cobalt and chromium, on which major industries depend.

Recent polls show that today, unlike the past, the majority of Americans do not see the world of the future as bright and promising. They see it staying the same or getting worse.

Add to this that citizens are increasingly skeptical of politics and government and more apathetic about voting, and the government administrator is facing a serious problem. Government officials at all levels will have to try to reassess the citizen's relationship to government and try to rebuild confidence in government by efficiently performing mutually agreed upon public goals. This book has attempted to help local public administrators find ways to meet these challenges.

[4] "The Global 2000 Report to the President: Entering the 21st Century." Washington, D.C.: U.S. GPO, 1980.

INDEX